UNLEASHED LEADERSHIP

Maximizing Talent & Performance by Opening the Gates of Opportunity

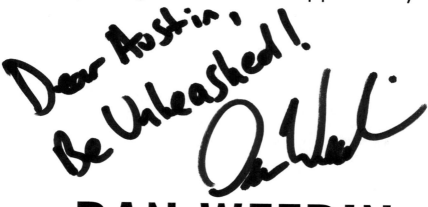

Dear Austin,
Be Unleashed!

DAN WEEDIN

KITSAP
PUBLISHING

Unleashed Leadership:
Maximizing Talent & Performance by
Opening the Gates of Opportunity

First edition, published 2015

By Dan Weedin

Cover design by Fusion Creative Works

ISBN 978-1-942661-11-5

Published by Kitsap Publishing
19124 Jensen Way NE
P.O. Box 1269
Poulsbo, WA 98370
www.KitsapPublishing.com

Printed in the United States of America

TD 20150921

100-10 9 8 7 6 5 4 3 2 1

Contents

Foreword

I'm not a lifelong learner, but rather a constant learner. I live in a world of ongoing amazement. For me, "spirituality" means identifying with the world around me and contributing to it as I learn from it, a symbiosis with nature.

Consequently, I've lived with dogs for a long time! I find them more than just companions, but rather sources of inspiration. They run through open gates without doing a needs analysis or risk/reward assessment. They are filled with delight that the yard is still there in the morning. They chase things animate and inanimate for the love of the chase.

And, preternaturally, they seem to know what's coming, whether it's the UPS driver with biscuits in a pocket or a distant thunderstorm.

Dan Weedin loves dogs, so he is part of this symbiotic life. I've had the pleasure to work with him for some time. I urged him continually to write about his insights and experiences. He, too, seems to know what's coming, so he's someone worth watching, reading, and knowing.

Self-esteem is a deep and enriching well of resources for some, but a bare cupboard for others. It can be a wellspring of strength when tapped, or result in crashing failure when missing. Over my 30 years in executive and entrepreneurial coaching, I've found this the single greatest factor in success or lack thereof—more so than capital, or experience, or contacts, or even originality.

The greatest leap of faith many of us have to make is to believe in ourselves, to trust in our own judgment, to be sanguine about our smarts. The secret to grand success is the synergy of high self-worth, dynamically increasing skill sets, and continuing passion. Michelangelo, when asked how he carved The David from a single piece of discarded marble, supposedly replied, "I carved away everything that didn't look like David." Thus, an eternal work of art was created.

We all have to "carve away" everything that we are not great at (or can become great at) and don't have passion for. That's why making money is only a byproduct. We need to find our passion and then make money, not make money and become passionate about it. The former is a rewarding life, the latter is an eternal march through stress, ulcers, and lack of fulfillment.

When we successfully carve away all but our great strengths and passion, we have the artwork of our careers and lives.

Dan Weedin is your sculpting instructor, your art advisor, your career coach. He knows where you are because he's been there, but he also has the instinct to know what's coming. He helps on the strategic level to design your (and your business's) future, and on the tactical level to determine how best to achieve it. He can "unleash" you not only to improve your own career, profession, or business, but also enable you to help others in your professional and personal life.

This book has arrived at a great time for you, because no matter what stage of growth you currently occupy, Dan will help you to grow further and faster. He creates positive change with positive psychology, but also creates sustainable results through the mastery of the skills and behaviors required for ongoing success. Make no mistake, this isn't a "self-help" book. You need Dan's help, as so many others have.

Congratulations for starting this journey. Enjoy it, exploit it, engage in it. You're about to run freely and energetically through the open gate.

~ **Alan Weiss, PhD**

*Author, **Million Dollar Consulting**,*
***Million Dollar Maverick**, and*
60 other books in 12 languages

Acknowledgments

I want to thank several people for their role in helping me be Unleashed in my own career and in writing this book. My sincere thanks go to my publisher, Ingemar Anderson; cover designer, Shiloh Schroeder; and editor, Bethany Brengan. I'm grateful for your trust and help.

I wouldn't be where I am today after ten years on my own as a consultant, speaker, and author without the extensive help of my professional mentor, Alan Weiss. I've been working with Alan personally since 2008, and his guidance, support, and *tough love* have been exactly what I have always needed to push forward in the right direction. From his community, I've been blessed to work closely with many people too numerous to mention. That being said, special thanks go to Noah Fleming, Libby Wagner, Roberta Matuson, Jean Oursler, Gary Patterson, Rick Pay, Betsy Jordyn, John Martinka, and Laurent Duperval.

Finally, my family has been unbelievably supportive of all my hare-brained, crazy, and sometimes irrational ventures. I am indebted to them for their patience, perseverance, and love. Thanks to my wonderful daughters, Mindy and Kelli. I love you both. And to my lovely, talented, supportive, and immensely tolerant wife of nearly thirty years, Barb. . . all I can say is thank you and I love you, *Esposita*. You've been the star in my life, and I am looking forward to many more adventures together.

Introduction

UNLEASHING THE POWER OF YOUR STAR

Sirius is the brightest star in the night sky. Its name is derived from the ancient Greek (meaning "glowing" or "scorcher"). Both Sirius's intrinsic luminosity and its nearness to earth make it appear so intense. Sirius is known colloquially as the "Dog Star," a nickname that reflects its prominence in its constellation, Canis Major (Greater Dog). In ancient times, the appearance of Sirius marked the flooding of the Nile for Egyptians and the "dog days" of summer for the Greeks. That was well before any of us were toiling in our "dog days of summer" of July and August! According to an astrological definition, "The Dog Star is a symbol of power, will, and steadfastness of purpose, and exemplifies the One who has succeeded in bridging the lower and higher consciousness."[1]

So why is this noteworthy? Dogs have been around as long as we humans have, as far as I can tell. I doubt they have changed much over the course of several centuries. In fact, I bet dogs have changed less than us and that may just be to their benefit. The definition of the Dog Star emphasizes terms like prominence, power, will, and steadfastness, which also define man's best friend. These are all virtues that we can use as leaders, wouldn't you agree?

Dogs don't wait at open gates, ruminating over past experiences, fears of the unknown, or whether they are making the right decision or not. They boldly attack adventure and opportunity. Human leaders often agonize over decisions, both small and large. Unfortunately, all too often we overthink, undervalue, and miss opportunities to improve ourselves, those we lead, and the organizations we work for. Bottom line: we would do well to add a little

[1] Karima Lachtane, "Canis Major," *History of Astrology* (blog), September 11, 2006, http://historyofastrology.blogspot.dk/2006/09/history-of-astrology-page-3-canis.html.

more power, will, and steadfastness of purpose to our lives.

This book is written for business leaders who, like adventurous dogs, strive to be "unleashed." Unleashed to discover their own strengths and talents. Unleashed to guide others to discover theirs. Unleashed to live life without regret, knowing they left no talent on the table.

You will find my partner in writing to be my epigrammatic and precocious dog, Captain Jack. He's been hanging out, helping me write, for many years now. His fans think he's better than me and deserves a raise. I figure his free food, free rent, and free health care gig is pretty good. He's not complaining. He and I both hope you enjoy his anecdotes at the end of each chapter. Thanks to him and his sidekick, Bella the Diva, I always have good stories!

So now it's time to get "Sirius" and read this book. I promise that you will find at least a few very valuable strategies, tactics, and concepts that you can immediately implement in both your professional and personal life to help you grow as a leader and as a human being. My genuine hope for you is that you will be Unleashed to maximize your own talents and the talents of those in your world.

The gate is now open. . .

~ **Dan Weedin**
Poulsbo, WA
March 2015

The Significant State of Mind

SIGNIFICANCE STARTS WITH YOU

To love oneself is the beginning of a lifelong romance.

~ Oscar Wilde

Not long ago, I was meeting with a new mentoring client and we were discussing his move into the world of consulting. He made a comment that really captured my attention. He said, "Dan, I have always been successful, however we define that. I'm at a point in my life where I want to be *significant*."

Wow.

The word *significant* has tremendous *significance*. It seems to me that when we start aging into midlife, the issue of being more than *successful* begins to seep into our consciousness.

What does being significant mean?

My definition is simple. *Being significant means making a meaningful contribution to the success and/or happiness of another human being.* I strive to be significant to my wife, to my daughters, to my extended family, to my friends, to my clients, and to my community. That means more than merely being in the room. It means offering something of compelling value—love, concern, opportunity, teaching, experience, wisdom, and hope.

My definition of success is that it is self-absorbed. In other words, people who are seeking success do so because it is to their personal benefit. When you're successful in building a business, writing a book, becoming an entrepreneur, or earning that corner office with the view, then you've personally achieved, and you are deemed "successful" by others and yourself. You have reached a pinnacle of sorts, and your income and lifestyle reflect that.

We are inundated with this mad clamor to become *successful* in our careers, in our marriages, in our relationships, yet this still points back to us personally, doesn't it? And when we are just getting started, this is what we want to attain. For many young people, the focus and responsibility are entirely all on one's self. It's not until we add other people (e.g., spouses, significant others, children, clients, employees, etc.) and a few bloodied knees called "experience" into the equation that mere money and power are viewed in a different light. Or at least they should be.

What does being significant mean to you?

This chapter will focus on how being significant is not about your accomplishments, but rather how you've made a positive impact on the lives of others. This might be personally or professionally. In the end, if you're providing value to a business, company, or organization, you are providing value to the people in that place. My hope is that as you consider this difference, you will start seeking significance over success, and in so doing, unleash yourself and those around you.

Are You Talking to Me?
Being Significant Starts With Your Self-talk

Being a leader means building a foundation. One of the masters of this concept was the late, legendary UCLA men's basketball coach, John Wooden. Coach Wooden admitted that he always started each year by teaching his players how to put on their socks and shoes before they even touched a basketball. Here is an excerpt from an ESPN interview where he was asked if he really did this:

Absolutely. I picked that up when I was teaching in high school. We had a lot of blisters, and I found out that a lot of the players didn't smooth out all the wrinkles around their heels and around their little toes, places where the blisters are apt to occur. Then I found out that they didn't lace their shoes properly and oftentimes they wore shoes that were a size too large.

With all the quick-stop turning, changes of direction, changes of pace on a hard floor you have in basketball, this would cause blisters. So, I thought it was very important that I'd check their shoe size and how they put their socks on. I hoped they would take a few extra seconds to smooth out the wrinkles around the heel and the toes and hold the sock up while they put their shoe on. I think it was important. And I know from the time I started in high school that we greatly reduced the number of blisters that we'd have, so I continued that throughout my coaching. I know a number of players laughed about it. They probably still laugh about it now. But I stuck to it. I think to some degree it helped team unity. I believed in that and I insisted on it.[2]

Coach Wooden believed in laying a foundation. If you put your socks and shoes on the right way, you avoid blisters. If you avoid blisters, you avoid injuries. When you avoid injuries, you get to play. When your best players play, then you win. Bottom line is that by doing the small things at the base level, you are more likely to enjoy success and significance.

The foundation of being influential always starts at the sock and shoe level, too. Except this isn't about your feet; it's about your brain. More specifically, it's what you say to yourself and how you say it.

None of us would ever accept insulting words and angry tones of voice from someone else, regardless of who they are. You wouldn't allow yourself to be cursed at or degraded. In fact, you might get very defensive and indignant, or you might just crawl into a shell and be withdrawn. But on some level, you would know that the other person's behavior was unreasonable. Yet that is exactly the sort of behavior many of us subject ourselves to on a

---

2   John Wooden, "Ten Burning Questions for. . .John Wooden," interview with Page 2, ESPN. com, 2001, http://espn.go.com/page2/s/questions/wooden.html.

daily basis. Our inner voice and words, our self-talk, can either be encouraging or destructive. In order to be influential and lead others, you'd better start by taking care of your own shoes and socks first.

Here's my personal example. I am prone to get angry with myself, and there is nothing wrong with that. When we make mistakes, it's natural to be frustrated with our behavior or missteps. But I know I've many times been guilty of inwardly saying, "Idiot." I wouldn't allow anyone else to call me "idiot," yet I'm pretty lax about saying it to myself. While this and other name-calling may seem trite, the reality is that we can regularly be bullies to ourselves. The results are no better, and probably worse, than being bullied by someone else. If you're going to lay a strong foundation to inspire and lift up others to maximize their skills and talents, start with what you say to yourself. If you don't believe in yourself, nobody else will.

The first step is identifying that you bully yourself. Once you've done that, you can begin the correction process. Let's make this simple: cut yourself come slack. Don't be so hard on yourself. You perfectionists out there, remember that you are human and prone to mistakes. Learn to laugh and not take yourself so seriously. And have some perspective that in the world we live in, mistakes will always be made because we're human. In business, few decisions are fatal. You can be resilient and recover and thrive out of the vast majority of them. If you keep that perspective, then you can start talking to yourself in a much more positive manner.

What's My Yard?
Avoiding the Insidious Trap Called "Complacency"

Success is a trap lying in wait. We began this chapter discussing the theory and mindset of the word *success*. If we work hard, do the right things, and never quit, we will ultimately earn that success we so desperately crave. The reason it's a trap is because the worst thing that can happen to any business leader, executive, entrepreneur, or professional is that they attain success and get snared by it and lie wasting away in "The Success Trap" for the rest of their career. Let's avoid this by determining how to make the most out of our yard.

4

Let's first define exactly what "The Success Trap" is so you will know it when you trip over it. My professional coach and mentor, Alan Weiss, introduced the concept of The Success Trap in his work with solo practitioner consultants. It works with any business leader or professional, not just consultants. Here is how Alan defines it:

> The "success trap" occurs when you are rewarded and lauded for something that you're good at but actually dislike. This is how jobs get in the way of careers, and necessary evils come to impede our lives. Let your internal gyroscope tell you what's right for you, not external influences.[3]

It starts after you've realized a measure of success. Let's say you're in sales of some sort—insurance, real estate, industrial siding, etc. You started out on your journey and could allocate all of your time to marketing and selling. You soaked in new knowledge like a sponge. And you received accolades for your rapid rise in the organizational ranks. You went from "garage band" to "rock star" at record speed (more on this later in the book)!

Of course, as you gained success, your commitments also increased. Now you started getting clients that needed attention. Your customer service work increased. You found yourself toiling behind your desk more and out in the field (doing what you most enjoyed) far less. You became known as a consummate professional who was good at doing the hard work for the client. You became a fixture in the office, chatting it up at the water cooler and (here's the slippery slope) becoming *comfortable*. Comfortable in your income, comfortable in your effort, comfortable in your results, and comfortable in your "success." Now instead of "rock star," you begin sounding like a well-used pair of shoes.

The trap becomes steeper at the next stage. I call this the "fear phase." Once you've gained comfort in all those things I mentioned, you suddenly start becoming fearful of getting out of this sandbox to play in the "real world" again. I liken it what happened to my golf game. When I was in high school, I was a competitive golfer. I was a two-year letter winner and com-

---

3   Alan Weiss, *Life Balance: How to Convert Professional Success into Personal Happiness* (San Francisco: Jossey-Bass/Pfeiffer, 2003), 226–7.

peted at the state level. For the next four to five years through college and into my early business career, my game was consistent and improved. Then I started having less time to play due to family and work commitments. I was comfortable in my game and spent less time practicing. What grew out of this was a fear of failure. In my youth, I was fearless. I never thought about hitting a stray shot or missing a putt. I was focused on achievement and prosperity, regardless of the odds. As I got more *comfortable*, I actually became more fearful of mistakes. Wayward shots and poor putts became my enemy. Instead of thinking positively, I focused on negative outcomes. I started playing it *safe* for fear of inflating my score. Counterintuitively, my score went up as I became more conservative.

The Success Trap has the same effect on your career "game." Once you're mired in the office and comfortable with your position, going out and being fearless doesn't come as easily. Just like I was skittish about hitting my ball out of bounds off the first tee, so business professionals imprisoned in the Success Trap fear rejection, bad breaks, poor performance, answering tough questions, being vulnerable, and most of all, being "found out." And like my golf score, the conservative and fearful route never leads to better success, just more penalty strokes!

Extra Point: If you think the acronym CEO translates into *über*-confidence, think again. There is a common ailment among CEOs where they worry they just aren't good enough, that they will be found out, that their subordinates will be disappointed in them. This thinking comes about when you're firmly ensnared in the trap.

So how do we avoid or get out of this greenside bunker Success Trap? Here is my five-step process to avoiding this malady:

1. **Self-Awareness**. Understand that this can happen to you. I encounter too many people who falsely believe they are impervious

to getting trapped. They cite experience, knowledge, and entre-preneurial dexterity as reasons. It's akin to not using a blind-spot detector in your car. You've always backed up, so why would you ever need any additional help? Being humble enough to recognize your vulnerabilities is always the foundation for building true awareness.

2. **Get Help.** You can't be brilliant by yourself. Strategic and intro-spective work is better when shared with someone who is skilled at coaching or mentoring. Just like working out at a gym with a professional trainer will maximize your improvement, working with a coach or mentor will unleash your maximum potential. This also involves vulnerability and real self-confidence, and the return on investment is huge.

3. **Change.** If you always do what you always did, you will always get what you always got. Without change, stagnation rules the day. Change for the sake of change doesn't work. Change needs to be intentional, strategic, and built around improving your condition. It's often hard, maybe even painful at the start. Yet if it's the correct strategy, then change will be the force that pulls you out of the pit!

4. **What's Your LIKE?** If you're doing something you dislike just because you're competent at it, then you're not maximizing your unique skill set. These dislikes might include processing orders, running errands, playing receptionist, doing your own book-keeping, and making the coffee in the morning. All are im-portant tasks for a well-oiled business, but not necessarily to be done by you. Delegate. Train. Desist. Eighty percent of your day should involve you doing things that only you can do AND that you like doing (e.g., marketing, selling, strategy, mergers and acquisitions, and brand building). If you dislike something that can be done by someone else, or that no longer needs to happen, make that change.

5. **Drop Weights and Toss Baggage.** If you're the executive or entrepreneur, or maybe the key player for your team, you will constantly need to drop "weight." Some things you once did can be delegated. You will find time being spent on activities that are no longer relevant and are still being done for no good reason. I bet some of you may still be dealing with obnoxious customers, toxic business partners, or needy people. You need to divorce yourself from people and things that drag you down and attack your time and spirit. That's when you're most susceptible to being trapped.

The first assessment is with you. As a leader and influencer of others, you must also be able to recognize the Success Trap in your team. Do you have direct reports, key employees, or sales pros that exhibit signs of complacency? I know when I worked for different organizations that complacent people were as obvious as a ham sandwich to a hungry teenage boy. If you allow them to continue down this path, two things happen (and both are bad). First, you lose production, performance, and money from these people. You're not getting all you can out of them. The results (or lack thereof) are a drain to the company. Second, you tell the rest of your employees that this behavior is acceptable. You actually create a culture of apathy and complacency. Falling into holes is easy; digging your way out of them, not so much. Avoiding this trap altogether is the way to go, and as a leader of people, that's your job.

Extra Point: The Success Trap is not limited to your professional career. Take a long and hard look at your personal life. Ever feel like you're stuck in a rut with your spouse, your kids, your daily life, or any other myriad of associations and groups you belong to? Every mid-life crisis ever conceived is undoubtedly a Success Trap in hiding. As you read through this chapter, don't just consider your career and job. Think about how these concepts may just parallel with your entire life.

Resilient Positivity
The "Next Play" Mentality

The word *resilient* is defined in the following way when applied to a person: ". . .recovering easily and quickly from shock, illness, hardship, etc. Irrepressible."

Irrepressible. What a great word to describe resilient. We think of resiliency just as it is defined. Something happens to someone, and they have the fortitude to bounce back and overcome, to rise like the Phoenix out of the ashes. If only it were as simple as it sounds.

In February 2014, my mom went into the hospital to deal with reoccurring issues with pulmonary effusions, or to simplify things for all of you non-medical readers, water accumulating in her lungs. At eighty-nine years old and in failing health due to the ravages of dementia, she physically didn't have much left to fight with. These effusions were sapping her of her strength and taxing her emotionally.

After an initial visit from the doctor, it was decided that she needed to have this water drained again. This is a grueling procedure for most people, and Mom, at 4' 10" and all of ninety-two pounds, really suffered when she had to have this done. My wife Barb and I had gone home to take a break. I had made the decision to return to the hospital that night, as Mom was due to have the draining procedure done at 8 p.m. I didn't want her to go through this alone, yet the procedure didn't require both of us there. I insisted that Barb stay at home.

After visiting Mom briefly, I had a private discussion with the doctor on duty. She started giving me confusing information about these effusions: "These effusions are a by-product of a heart problem she is having. She's already had several episodes. I don't think she will leave the hospital alive." You see, Mom had a Do Not Resuscitate (DNR) on file. If she went through a cardiac arrest and I wasn't there, the hospital would have no choice but to allow her to die.

As I was still wrestling with this new information, the doctor who had come to do the effusion procedure became concerned. Mom was getting increasingly agitated and scared. I started texting Barb about what was going on. She asked, "Do you want me to come?" I said, "No. I think it's fine for now." No sooner than I hit SEND, then a whirlwind began. Mom went into a cardiac arrest. She was dying right in front of me. The doctor looked at me and asked me something I will never forget. . .

"Do you want us to try to save her?"

Because I had power of attorney, I had the capacity to authorize life-saving measures. It took me about two seconds to say, "YES!" In my view, we would either save her and she would get another chance, or she would die with us trying. I was prepared for both outcomes. Over the next twenty minutes (which seemed like two hours), I watched Mom being given the defibrillator and CPR by this doctor and a group of valiant nurses. Their efforts were not in vain. She stayed the night in intensive care, where we were again told that there was still a more than 50 percent chance that she would pass away while in the hospital.

I still recall the priest who came to give her last rites, just in case. He asked her, "Alicia, are you ready to meet Jesus?" She answered, "Yes, but not now." He chuckled. After a few more minutes, he asked again, "Alicia, are you ready to meet Jesus?" Her answer (with a little added emphasis), "Yes, but not now." He tried one more time, and she looked at him as if he must be deaf. Her response was the same. He smiled, looked at us, and said, "She's not dying yet. She's not ready to go."

Mom lived for almost another two years. Resilient. Irrepressible. Significant.

That's my definition of "resilient." It's that powerful capability to bounce back after a trauma of any kind—physical or emotional. Now let's combine this with "positivity."

It's not human to be ceaselessly positive. Bad things happen to all of us that will alter our attitudes and often our worldviews. My experience tells me that it's most often the small setbacks over time that have the most effect on a person's attitude and mentality. While Mom's story was pretty dramatic to her and to us, I feel like we all go through some trial or tribulation virtually daily and that these add up to affect our thinking.

Being positive sounds easy, and it is when things are wonderful. In fact, it's really easy to be a terrific leader of a business or company when the sun is shining. But as collegiate basketball coach James Harrison "Babe" McCarthy once quipped, "The sun don't shine on the same dog's butt every day." And it don't. . . er, doesn't!

Showing resilient positivity is similar to a good stock on the New York Stock Exchange or NASDAQ. There will be occasional dips over time. Stock traders will often cash in on gains or sometimes a little bad news affects the stock. However, those dips never go too deep or last too long before the stock starts trending up again. That's got to be you.

First, you need to develop an attitude of being positive. Much of the remainder of this book will focus on that. The next step is the most critical. It's finding a way to be resilient when things look bleak. You need some perspective and some internal trigger to provide you with the very best self-talk you can muster. Sure, it is great to have coaches, colleagues, mentors, and family to help you talk about things, and that can't be overstated. Yet in the end, it's about you and the determination that regardless of the reason for the "dip," you will correct your "stock" to start trending back in the right direction.

Being resiliently positive is easy to say and much more difficult to do. As you read this book, keep this concept in mind as we discuss important strategies and tactics for achieving this mentality so that you can be an Unleashed leader.

The Invisible Fence
Breaking Down Barriers for Yourself and Others

As a dog owner, I've toyed with the idea of installing an invisible fence. Our house does have a spacious backyard. The issue is that it backs up to an open greenbelt, and our property line starts falling back into that area. This makes it almost impossible to actually fence our yard and not cut off a chunk of our property.

We have friends that swear by their invisible fence. None of them own a Jack Russell terrier. I've watched Captain Jack bolt out of doors and "Houdini" his way out of a harness. A quick bolt of electricity wouldn't stop him, even if he knew it was coming! (Captain Jack's observations on the invisible fence are at the conclusion of this chapter.)

I believe that we as humans actually construct our own "invisible fences" around ourselves as some sort of "protection," yet in reality they become a self-imposed incarceration. Captain Jack very eloquently describes this in his missive, so I will talk about the best way to overcome this.

This is how you build an invisible fence in your life: You construct it link by link with distractions and negative talk, and in so doing, talk yourself out of being Unleashed. Consider this diagram illustrating the 5 Lethal Links of Your Invisible Fence:

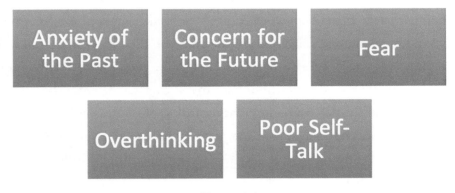

Figure 1.1

Lethal Link #1—Anxiety of the Past

These are your past mistakes. It's the concept of "once bitten, twice shy." These anxieties keep you arms-length or more from trying anything remotely similar to your last failure for fear of being hurt again (that can mean physically or emotionally). This is basically the collar around your neck that you know will shock you when you get too close to the edge!

As I mentioned earlier, I played competitive golf in high school. Our team was very good, as evidenced by our competing in the state championship my junior year. I remember one match being played at a really challenging and terrific golf course named Kayak Point. Trees surrounded Kayak Point, and I always seemed to have trouble avoiding them! However, on this day, I played a brilliant front nine. I was tied for third at the turn and excited about my prospects for a high finish for the team and me. I was hungry, so I picked up and wolfed down a hot dog before teeing off on hole ten. The back nine was brutal for me. After a forty on the front, I ballooned to a fifty-five on the back, which gave me a score well above my regular game and out of contention. I blamed it on the hot dog. I'm not kidding. For years, I figured that eating during my round was going to magically cause me to play poorly. It was as if a wizard straight out of *Harry Potter* had cast a spell on all sustenance in an effort to waylay my good golf scores. I eventually overcame this by realizing I was perfectly capable of playing badly all on my own.

While this might seem like a kooky example, I bet you can find some of your own wacky ones. We get these bad experiences in our heads and believe that ALL future ones will end up the same. In the end, that is both unreasonable and unfair to ourselves. And it costs us being our best.

Lethal Link #2—Concern for the Future

My wife is brilliant. I really married up. She is the calming influence of our family and balances out my zaniness to make sure we are always moving in the right direction. That being said, if she has a small (and I mean really small) flaw, she would admit to being a worrier. Any time we would prepare to leave our house for the day, an expedition would be sent to ensure that no door was unlocked, no appliance left on, and nothing plugged in, in any bathroom. This has never been a cursory look—that would be normal. This is a comprehensive analysis with redundancies that would make the most fervent technology company proud. And as we would finally start down the road, the inevitable question still comes: "Did you check to see if I unplugged my curling iron?"

We can get so consumed with worry about negative things that might happen that we lose perspective and create a lethal link to taking risks. My completely unscientific data tells me that 97.3 percent of all bad things we conjure up in our heads simply never occur. Your data is probably similar.

Don't allow uncertainty and fear to become a barrier. Being prudent is fine. Prudence to a level of dread and panic is simply unhealthy and will leave you stuck in your yard muttering to yourself.

Lethal Link #3—Fear

Fear is the common denominator for most of these concepts. The first two links are perfect examples: fear of a return of pain and fear of the unknown causing pain. However, fear doesn't have to be that blatant. I have seen even minor levels of fear paralyze some of the most sophisticated business leaders.

When I was a young insurance agent, I considered myself pretty fearless. I was gregarious, loquacious, and brimming with confidence. Yet I found myself often playing it safe for fear of not landing a new account, or losing a current one. You see, when you're paid on commission, you eat what you kill. With a young family to care for, I had concerns about making sure I had some of that "kill" on the dinner table. I would lose track of the value I was providing to my clients and make decisions or say things based on not upsetting the applecart. In retrospect, I bet I ended up losing more opportunities because this thinking kept me from getting outside my comfort zone and finding new clients and developing stronger relationships.

Here is an exercise for you to do:

Look back on your last twelve months of decisions, both personal and professional. Yes, I know you made an incalculable number of decisions in a year, but play along. You likely recall the most important. How many times did you avoid taking a bold risk or implementing an organizational change and just played it safe out of fear? How many of those decisions might you now change if fear of failure or rejection were removed?

Lethal Link #4—Overthinking

I work closely with a lot of really smart people (and that's not just because they hired me!). The most common remark I make to all of them is that they are overthinking a problem or situation. I can do this because I've had great practice myself as an overthinker! At least now I know what to look for in myself.

Overthinking rears its head when we need to justify a decision. It is really rooted in fear of one of the items previously mentioned. The fear of failure, fear of rejection, or fear of being found out can lead to analysis paralysis. This is a common link in many an "invisible fence" we humans have.

My experience is that overthinking is hard to overcome on your own. You need someone to help you identify when you do it. One of my biggest helpers is a colleague of mine whom I have an accountability partnership with. Noah does a terrific job of saying, "Dan, you're overthinking. Just do it the best you can, commit, and move on." The irony is that I do the same for him. It's much easier for us to give that "tough love" to each other because we aren't tied to the results. However, in a partnership like this, we do have a personal investment in the success of the other, so the guidance we can give to stop overthinking is genuine.

The best way to avoid building this chain of links is to find someone who will help you realize when you're overthinking, someone whom you are willing to share ideas with and get help from when needed. When you do this, over time, you get better at self-diagnosing "overthink," and you're free to venture outside the gate more often and much quicker!

Lethal Link #5—Poor Self-Talk

Sound familiar? I won't reiterate this discussion as we covered it already. Just know it's a part of this chain.

How to Stay in the Moment

The one single most important thing I may have ever learned from Alan Weiss is this: You must stay in the moment. As a young professional, I allowed all of the things I listed above to keep me fenced in. Once I truly understood what I was doing on my own volition and the damaging results, both personally and professionally, I took a path to making changes.

Extra Point: There is a legendary "cowboy anthem" written by Cole Porter and Robert Fletcher, and immortalized by the great Roy Rogers, called "Don't Fence Me In." The song extols the American West's desire to be free to roam the countryside, sleep under the stars, and "listen to the murmur of the cottonwood trees," without being saddled by anyone or anything. It's a tranquil and utopian dream that permeated American ideology in the mid-twentieth century after the Great Depression rocked the country. That ideal eventually gave way to industry, business, and a fast-paced lifestyle. In a sense, we Americans "fenced ourselves in" with increased stress, anxiety, and obligation. I wonder if we can find our way back to a simpler ideal from the past that allows us to "roam free" in the career and lifestyle of our own choosing.

Staying "in the moment" sounds easier than it actually is. Our mind digests gazillions of thoughts in seconds, and just one of those thoughts can sabotage a project, a conversation, or a behavior. So how do you improve in this one critical area of self-discipline?

My background is in risk and crisis management. Ironically, you are risking being in a crisis when you leave "the moment" in a business setting! There are five steps to the risk management process for any business. They are identification of risk, analysis around those risks and exposures, control to avoid future calamity, methods of financing catastrophe, and implementation and monitoring. Don't worry. This isn't going to be a lesson in risk and crisis management. However, these five methods translate to staying focused on what's in front of you.

Here are my **5 Methods for Staying in the Moment**:

1. *Identify* what distracts you. For me, one of my biggest is a visual stimulus. That's why I have to work hard at keeping my desk area uncluttered. If I see things that distract me, I lose focus.

Email notifications also divert my attention, so I increased the time between email notifications to one hour to avoid having constant temptations of interruptions. What about you? If you were to honestly assess and identify what distracts you, what would be the biggest culprits?

2. *Analyze* those areas you've identified. I'm not talking about launching a "formal investigation" that will eat up your time and become its own distraction. Take thirty minutes and find out why these things pull you away from the moment. For example, if you find yourself in conversation and you are already thinking ahead to what your response is going to be while the other person is talking, then you're out of the moment. You identify this as a challenge. What's the reason for it?
   When you find your mind racing ahead in conversations, it's because you have an agenda. It might be to consummate a sale, to land a new job, to influence an employee or boss, or to convince your spouse of where to go on vacation. The problem is that you've stopped listening to the other person. There is opportunity for knowledge, growth, and influence when you stop trying to stay two steps ahead. If you identify this, analysis will crystallize the *why*.

3. *Control* what you can control. We can't control everything. Emergencies are never scheduled. When distractions occur that demand your attention, you have to deal with them. However, the vast majority of your distraction doesn't deal with crisis situations. It deals with areas you can control through self-discipline. Examples: If you're distracted by a messy workplace, clean it. If emails distract you, change the frequency of delivery. If you dominate conversations, stop talking (you will eventually *feel* this). If you are constantly running late, schedule yourself to leave your office earlier by actually marking it on your calendar and setting an alarm. None of this is probably new to you.

However, the implementation of it is hard. It requires a resolve and discipline that most people don't have the patience to follow through with.

4. *Get help.* You may have seen in my risk management example that the fourth method was "financing." This involves transferring your risk to someone else through contract (e.g., insurance). In my example for you, this is *transferring the accountability to someone else.* That's where mentoring and coaching comes in. The biggest conundrum we all have when it comes to behavior change is that we try to do it all on our own. That's why we often fail. We all need someone who will hold us accountable and be a voice of support.

   I suggest this be someone who is not a family member or friend. These people love you, want what's best for you, and yet often give you terrible advice. You need a professional colleague (from within your own company or a business group) or a professional coach who is willing to give you tough love and hold you accountable to your objectives and goals. You may ask, how does this help you stay in the moment? Coaching and accountability are key when looking to change behaviors, including learning to be in the moment. If this is an area of focus, then your conversations and activities will be diagnosed by your coach and you will be held accountable for them.

5. *Implement and Monitor.* The hardest part of the process. You've identified your areas of behavior that need to improve (distractions). You've analyzed why they are challenges to you. You have set up a system to control what you can and to get help. Now you simply have to implement the changes and work on them daily. The reason it's so hard is because it requires patience. I promise that with daily practice, you will suddenly catch yourself when you slip into old habits. Prior to this, you never noticed. Now is your opportunity to realize that you're talking

too much and you need to be focused on the other person. You realize that thoughts of the future distract you and you are not paying attention to what's in front of you, so you refocus.

Final example: I love walking my dogs in the evening. Summers are the best when it's still warm, the sun is starting to set, and there is quiet around the neighborhood. It's an opportunity for my mind to wander and sometimes start obsessing over "problems" in the future that may be out of my control. I can soon find myself spending the entire time unhappy about a situation that may never even arise. Ever happen to you? Instead, I pull myself back and "be" in the moment by realizing that this time of leisure and joy won't come again, not exactly like this. I need to embrace it not only physically (walking), but also mentally (enjoyment). When you do all the things I mentioned above, it's much easier to catch yourself in these moments and ultimately make the right corrections.

A Captain Jack Extra Point
The Cloak of Invisibility

Hello. My name is Captain Jack, and I'm the terribly charming, witty, and intelligent pal of my human, Dan. I've been observing human behavior and have come to the conclusion that you all can learn a lot from dogs. Especially me. You see, I'm a Jack Russell, and we are unquestionably the smartest dogs on the planet.

I love watching television. Barb and Dan seem to find it remarkable that my attention can be so focused on a TV program. I don't know why. If they can focus, I can probably do it even better. I'm a dog, after all.

We just got done binge watching all eight movies of the Harry Potter series. Kelli came home after college, and they're her favorite movies. Since Dan and Barb hadn't seen all of them, she convinced them it would be a fun family activity. Of course, I joined in on the watching. I was most impressed with the whole "cloak of invisibility" thing. You know the cool cloak that, when Harry hides under it, keeps him invisible? Imagine what I could do with that!

I know humans that put up a similar thing called "an invisible fence." The invisible fence is like the cloak concept. It hides the fence; except in this case, there is no fence! At least Harry Potter is underneath the cloak! Dan is smart enough to know I won't fall for that trick. Some dogs don't see it, but they've been trained by their humans through a form of "shock and pain therapy" to avoid going through the gate. If I had a few minutes with those dogs, I would teach them how to break free.

It's only a small amount of pain. You take off running hard at your destination, understand that you will get a quick blast of pain, but then you're free! Once you're "unleashed," you can move on and explore your options and gain new adventures and experiences.

Here is what some humans do: they act like those other dogs behind invisible fences. They think the hurt is fatal. They avoid taking that big run to their dreams. They stay in their yards doing whatever it is that they are doing and then get bored. If they only knew that great adventures and experiences are out on the horizon and that the little pain is part of that, they would do what I do.

Be like me. Know that in life you might have to take a little pain to get the results you want. "No pain, no gain" is what I've heard humans say about exercise. It's probably truer about life.

Just saying. . .
Captain Jack

Unleashing Your Articulation

LANGUAGE SKILLS ON STEROIDS

Our language is the reflection of ourselves. A language is an exact reflection of the character and growth of its speakers.

~ Cesar Chavez

My favorite author is Edgar Allan Poe. I'm not sure what it is about his stories and style that have made him my esteemed writer, yet he is. Upon her high school graduation and departure for college, my daughter Mindy gave me a book of Poe's entire work. I've avidly reread many of the short stories and poems over and over.

One of the things I notice from Poe is his prodigious use of language. His work was popular in the mid-nineteenth century in America. The language isn't meant to be flowery or pretentious. Its purpose is to help the reader visualize, feel, smell, and be engaged in the moment. Its intent is to help the reader fully understand the mind of the narrator (most of Poe's work involves first person accounts).

My vocabulary is better because of reading Edgar Allan Poe. That results in being a better writer, speaker, and communicator. I fear we are living in an age where "dumbed down" applies to language. This generation has more books to read and more ways to read them than ever before, yet the imagery and imagination invented by writers like Poe, Ernest Hemingway, and John Steinbeck seem to have vanished.

The result of this is that our communication itself is not as vast. We speak and communicate as we write and read. Technology has exacerbated the situation by making it easier for us to broadcast our thoughts via sound bites. We use more words to describe; we use less powerful and more mundane language; and we put a premium on bland over brilliant. Poe is probably rolling over in his grave.

Why is this important? The ability to influence is stimulated by shaping emotion. Words are powerful catalysts to elicit those emotions. Logic makes people think, and emotions make them act. If you want to be influential as a leader, a sales professional (which is a role many of you leaders will still have), or elocutionist, then the more pithy and powerful your language, the better.

You don't have to come across as ostentatious. You need to have a sense of the appropriate time and place. However, you never need to "dumb down" your language in a professional setting. The default assumption should be that everyone in the room is smart and will understand sound use of the language. While there may be occasions where clarification is needed, doing so will only be to the benefit of everyone.

Here's the deal, folks. In order to be truly influential and Unleashed as a leader, your message must be clear, concise, powerful, and in many cases, game changing. You have to get people to "move," whether they be employees, board members, investors, clients, prospective clients, or community members. Language is the cornerstone to your success, and just because you have the ability to open your mouth and gush forth words and sentences, doesn't mean you are influential. This chapter will help make you so.

As Alan Weiss has declared, "Language controls discussion; discussion controls relationships; and relationships control business." Consequently, language controls business.

Words have no power to impress the mind without the
exquisite horror of their reality.

~ Edgar Allan Poe

Strategic Language
The Mission and Vision of Being Influential

Having a broad vocabulary and being persuasive is more than merely being a loquacious "pitchman." So many business professionals I have worked with personally have lamented that they could never spit out the words that they wanted to say at the right moment. In part, it's because of poor planning. Many business leaders don't take ample time to actually visualize a meeting and adequately plan and prepare their message. They take for granted that they will say the correct thing. On the opposite end, some leaders over-prepare and over-rehearse, eliminating spontaneity.

There are also some very human issues that arise for a leader dealing with a lack of influential language. Here are my three reasons for this lack:

- **Lack of Vocabulary.** The smaller the pond you're fishing in, the less fish will be available. Alternatively, the larger the lake, the greater the opportunity to catch the right fish at the right time. The small pond can be cramped and cluttered. The lake offers more adequate and unrestricted space for the fish to swim, thus making them easier to catch.
  So I'm not a fisherman, and my metaphor might be a bit skewed, but you get my point. The deeper your vocabulary, the more deftly you will be able to pluck out just the right word or phrase when you need it. Improve you vocabulary and enhance your improvisation.
- **Lack of Confidence.** When you're confident that you can hit the curveball, you are literally begging the pitcher to toss it. If you are afraid of the curveball, your chance of making contact is slim to none at best. If you lack confidence in your ability to

clearly respond with the appropriate words, then you are likely to go down with a "swing and a miss." How do you gain confidence? By improving and practicing your vocabulary.

The other negative result from lack of confidence is that you look and sound unsure and shaky, which you recognize and which only intensifies the situation for you.

- **Cluttered Brain.** Ah, to be in the moment with a clear head. Unfortunately, many a conflict and exchange have come at inopportune times and without warning. The uncertainty of the conversation can often fill your head with multiple scenarios played out at rapid speed while you're attempting to snag that perfect word or statement. Just like a cluttered office, garage, or inbox can become an obstacle to efficiency, so can a cluttered brain accelerate *mumbo jumbo* (this is the highly-evolved technical term for gibberish).

The obvious answer is to relax, have a clear mind, and be knowledgeable. The application is more onerous.

This chapter is about strategy. Part of your strategy should be clear improvement. Let's start with the words we use every day in an effort to persuade and inspire.

9 Techniques to Improve Your Vocabulary Fast

1. **Read**—This one is pretty elementary, yet often underused. The more you read, the better your vocabulary. Even if you abstained from doing any research on words you didn't know, just by reading them in the sentence, your level of knowledge will rise.

   Here are some scary facts:

   - In 1978, 42 percent of Americans said that they had read eleven or more books in the past year. That shrunk to 34 percent in 1990 and to just 23 percent in 2014.[4]
   - When surveyed, employers said they found 72 percent of

4   Jordan Weisman, "The Decline of the American Reader," *The Atlantic*, January 21, 2014, http://www.theatlantic.com/business/archive/2014/01/the-decline-of-the-american-book-lover/283222/. The author compares Pew and Gallop polls.

high school graduates "deficient" in writing in English.[5]

- Among college graduates, reading proficiency has declined 20 to 23 percent (between 1992 and 2003).[6]
- In 2014, 23 percent of Americans didn't read a single book.[7]

The bottom line is that we adults don't read as much as we once did. The reasons are pretty clear—television and technology. Television and the Internet too easily babysit us. In the 1940s, you could go to a movie, but that was about it. Even when I was a kid in the 1970s, the first television set I remember in my house had thirteen channels, and I had to stand up and change them manually. And we wonder why the language of Edgar Allan Poe trounces our own. . .

2. **Write**—I admit I don't write cursive any more other than to sign my name. I've relegated myself to printing only. While I know there is research that chronicles the value of cursive writing for the brain, I've kept to my new friend, the keypad. The result is I write. A lot.

While my career dictates that I write to create intellectual property and to market my business, I do enjoy it. That's probably why I'm in this career. The reality is that regardless of your career, you can write more. If like me, a good part of your work

5   National Endowment for the Arts, "To Read or Not to Read: A Question of National Consequence," November 2007, 16, http://arts.gov/sites/default/files/ToRead.pdf. Referencing The Conference Board, Corporate Voices for Working Families, Partnership for 21st Century Skills, Society for Human Resource Management, *Are They Really Ready to Work? Employers Perspectives on Basic Knowledge and Applied Skills of New Entrants to the 21st Century Workforce*, 2006.

6   National Endowment for the Arts, "To Read or Not to Read: A Question of National Consequence," November 2007, 14, http://arts.gov/sites/default/files/ToRead.pdf. Referencing statistics from the U.S. Department of Education.

7   Jordan Weisman, "The Decline of the American Reader," *The Atlantic*, January 21, 2014, http://www.theatlantic.com/business/archive/2014/01/the-decline-of-the-american-book-lover/283222/. Referencing a Pew survey.

requires writing, you have no excuse. If it doesn't, there are still ways to increase writing and thus improve your vocabulary:

- *Journal.* There are many forms of journaling, including gratitude journals, diaries, and keeping notebooks of inspirational quotes and sayings.
- *Blog.* Find a hobby or avocation and blog about it. It might be travel, cooking, sports, or kayaking. Whatever it is, blogging is basically free. You can write about things that excite you and share with the world.
- *Write a book.* Many do this for business use, yet others can do it simply for fun. Almost everyone I encounter has admitted that they'd like to write a book of some genre, related to business or not. Self-publish and share with your family. My dad was a genealogist for the last decade of his life, and he ended up writing his autobiography. It was shared with family only and became a treasure for all of us.
- *Poetry.* My colleague and friend Libby Wagner has made a career of using poetry as part of business. This is a very creative exercise for your brain and will not only help you become a better writer (and speaker), but also be a source of inspiration and relaxation.

3. **Use a Thesaurus**—Every time I write, I have my browser open to the online thesaurus. When I am writing, I can sometimes *feel* a certain word on the tip of my metaphorical tongue, but can't spit it out. A thesaurus quickly helps me locate it. Even better, my internal thesaurus expands. My mind becomes programmed for quickly sifting appropriate words when I'm speaking to others as well. The same will happen for you. If you write for any reason—books, articles, white papers, blogging, or social media—the constant use of a thesaurus will not only aid you in your project, but also help you grow in your ability to communicate orally.

4. **Look It Up**—If you're like me, you might wish you had a dollar for every time your parent or teacher would curtly respond to your question about a particular word's meaning with "Look it up in the dictionary!" I'm imploring you to do the same thing. I've made a habit of immediately seeking out a word's definition when I find one I don't recognize. This is a bit harder when reading a physical book. I generally have to look it up later. The advent of reading tablets like Kindle and Nook has uncomplicated and sped up the process. You can easily highlight a word and look it up within seconds. Taking just a brief time to do this will make a difference in your linguistic acumen. However, don't stop there. Now try to use that word in a conversation in the coming week! When you can actually apply something new, it will become more engrained in your memory bank and your likelihood of easy retrieval is improved.

5. **Play the Games**—My daughters and I have been competing with each other for years in two specific word games on our phones: Words with Friends and Hanging with Friends. Until recently, both girls went to school two thousand four hundred miles away from me. This was a great way for us to keep in touch through cyberspace. It also turned into a terrific tool to improve my vocabulary. In my competitive zeal to win games, I would try out new words (and always seek out their definitions), have new words used against me, and train my brain to uncover a variety of words. It's no secret that games have always been a device to improve our perspicacity and advance our knowledge and thinking skills. The advancement of technology has just made them easier to access and share.

6. **Join Toastmasters**—I'm a long-time member of this international organization that has devoted itself to helping people become better communicators and leaders. Toastmasters clubs around the world will challenge you to improve your vocabulary

through prepared speeches and extemporaneous speaking exercises. Toastmasters is inexpensive, easily accessible, and wildly successful if you give it your best effort.

7. **Learn Another Language**—The mere act of trying a new language will actually sharpen the skill of your native one. The exercises and effort to gain comprehension in an unfamiliar language puts an emphasis on defining words in your familiar tongue. Through that work, I believe you get a better vocabulary.

8. **Hire a Speech Coach**—Coaches can help you be accountable to your goals when you're not feeling committed. They have tools and techniques to help you develop your speaking ability, including an enhancement of your vocabulary.

9. **Social Media**—Hard to believe I would say this, but I think it's true. Social media is replete with people communicating. Twitter makes you be pithy (one hundred forty characters). Many other sites, like Facebook, might help you keep current on jargon and idioms that can come in handy. This isn't an excuse to troll social media all day. Just be cognizant as you read your social media feed of new words and opportunities to learn.

The mission and vision of being influential is getting the other person to take action. What is their call to action? If you can't elucidate that well enough, your mission will not be met. Strategy starts with being skilled and knowing your goal. Have a clear objective in mind for every interaction, whether it be a meeting with an employee on discipline, or with a prospective client on accepting your business proposal. You must have a plan and a call to action, and your vocabulary needs to be set up to deliver.

Tactical Language
The "How" of Being a Significant Influencer

Strategy is about planning and preparing. Tactics are about the implementation. Specifically, it's the manifestation of your strategy. With tactics only and no strategy, you have no vision or guidance. Strategy without tactics is just good ideas floating around in the air. You need both to move people and processes.

Here is my compilation of five how-to steps:

1. **Remove emotion from the equation**. You are probably thinking sarcastically, *Yeah, right. That's easy to do!* I am not suggesting that you be devoid of all emotion, especially passion for your message. However, in order to be heard and express that message, you must avoid the polar opposites of anger and exuberance. Both can be deadly to your efforts to influence. Focus on observed behaviors, valid data, and (this is the biggie) outcomes. How is your idea improving something? You can always accomplish this with a smile and sincere genuineness. Just avoid having your demeanor, rather than your idea, be the message.

2. **Avoid talking too much.** I can say this, as I am a recovering over-talker. This comes from a lack of confidence. That lack of confidence may be in yourself or in your message. Regardless, your excitement (many times my issue) or your anxiety will cause you to talk too much.

3. **Ask questions.** A lot. Questions are the key to your discussions. Hucksters and con men are noted for their verbosity of dialogue, barely able to take a breath in between sentences. The real pros in communicating are focused on asking great questions. Here's the hard part: you may need to come up with these on the fly! When I'm in situations (especially one-on-one sessions) where I am trying to be persuasive, I focus on two things. The first is staying in the moment (see the next step). The second is finding a way to change that "statement" I was about to foist on my unsuspecting companion and turn it into a question. Let's take a look at an example.

   Case Study: Your manager tells you, "Boss, there is no way we can meet that deadline. Our workers just aren't motivated enough and really don't care. I think we need to delay the project."

Response 1: *"Well, we need to fix that. I will call a full employee meeting and nip this negative thinking in the bud. We can't have that kind of nonsense around here!"*

Response 2: *"What evidence do you have that the employees lack motivation and don't care?"* (Then STOP, PAUSE, and LISTEN to the answer. The LISTEN action is the one that gets violated constantly!)

Response 2 is the better one because it is short without trying to "fix" the problem. It puts the onus back on the person making the statement. The rationale may be real; however, you must uncover it from them.

4. **Stay in the moment.** Have you ever gotten lost in the middle of a conversation when someone was talking because you became distracted by something? That "something" might have been your witty or biting response, or maybe someone you really wanted to talk to entered the room, or perhaps you began thinking about what you wanted for dinner that night. Regardless, you left the moment and now have no idea what was said.

One of the biggest challenges is that in conversation we are often either excited or agitated. We simply can't wait to get out our opinion and get back in the debate. This causes many problems: from misunderstandings, to guessing intent, to sheer rudeness.

Staying present is against human nature, in my opinion. It's just really hard to do when you have a strong desire to be influential, regardless of your personality style. You can lose being in the present even when not saying a word (note the daydreamers and doodlers among us).

Being present is a learned skill. The first step is to assess and understand when you begin losing the present. I know I can now tell. It's just a small feeling that enters my mind when more than one speaker (the second "speaker" is me) enters my brain. Once that understanding is achieved, then the next step is to snap yourself out of it. I always envision that scene in the 1987 movie *Moonstruck* where Cher slaps Nicolas Cage in the face and exhorts, *"Snap out of it!"*

After that, you need to simply focus on the other person. I focus on keeping eye contact. When you lose that all important engagement, it's easy to wander. Captain Jack loves to peer out the window for hours and can easily be distracted. Once we stop looking at the windows (the eyes) of the person we are supposed to focus on, we can become as distracted as my canine companion.

Finally, use questioning to confirm and clarify. That means you are staying focused and lets the other person know you care about his or her opinion.

5. **Avoid competition.** Tactically, we all want to compete and "win." It's another human nature thing. However, when conversations where you want to exert influence are at stake, you always lose when you try to win.

Influence is not about competition with another person. If you want to compete with yourself by meeting all the tactical goals you set, fine. But trying to win arguments becomes contagious, and your influence will drop, even if you get your way. Instead of trying to throw or hit the curveball, consider this a friendly game of badminton where the goal is to volley back and forth. Yes, I know badminton has winners and losers, but work with me. Being influential requires the tactical knowledge of seeking "win-win" situations.

What Did You Say?
How to Become an Exemplary Influential Listener

You've all heard the old saying. . .in order to be a good "teacher," you need to be a good listener. Being influential is, in a way, being a teacher. If you are in a position of influence, you must raise awareness, persuade, and "teach" the tricks of your trade to employees, as well as assisting customers and clients. The best way to do that is to be a good listener, or as I like to put it, an influential listener.

Extra Point: *¿Qué Dijo?* I was eating breakfast at a hotel in Somerset, NJ, getting ready to head back home after a long East Coast "tour." I heard my waitress speaking in Spanish with the hostess and an idea struck me. I was looking to improve my conversational Spanish. What a great way to practice: by speaking it with my waitress!

I asked her when she returned, and she graciously said she would be happy to speak to me in Spanish. The problem was that she didn't follow through. When I would talk to her in Spanish, she would respond to me in English. That doesn't help me. . . I'm pretty good in English! Now my Spanish is not so bad that she didn't understand; based on her responses, she did. After a few attempts, I just gave up and figured I would try it again sometime in the future.

My waitress heard me. I knew that because she acknowledged it. However, she wasn't *listening*. Listening takes the act of hearing and manifests it into a positive action. Had she been listening, she would have realized that my need was more than getting my bacon and eggs for breakfast. It was practicing my Spanish with her.

What do you hear, but not listen to?

We've all heard techniques for "active listening." I won't regurgitate them here because I'd like to simplify the process. I find that simplification isn't a "dumbing down" of the technique; rather it's assurance that the technique might actually be implemented.

If you want to become an influential listener, it really is a simple three-step process illustrated by this visual:

Influential Listening

Figure 2.1

These are in no particular order. They all need to be present. Here are my definitions for all three components:

Clean Mind: You have to remove the clutter. A few years ago, my garage was a disaster. It had become the holding tank for all my personal stuff, both before and after a couple decades-plus of marriage. It contained "stuff" that belonged to both daughters, and neither of them was living at home at the time. And it was beginning to accumulate items from my parents' household as they transitioned into a new reality. It was more than an eyesore for me. There were items in there I needed—tools, fixtures, mementos, and valuables. I struggled to find these things I needed (sometimes of an urgent nature), I had to buy new tools because I couldn't locate where I had (or even if I had) the old ones, and I had to constantly rearrange and move things to get to places where I needed to be. I had a broken water pipe, which added a lot of angst and stress to the whole situation. One summer, I knew this had to end, so I spent a weekend cleaning up, throwing away, shredding, and "uncluttering." It was a thorough and complete cleansing.

The result was a garage that was organized. This relieved stress, frustration, and anger. And I was able to put my car inside, which kept me out of the rain when leaving home!

You have to "clean" your mind when listening. We humans have a lot going on in our heads that distracts and clutters our brains. To be truly present, we need to intentionally cleanse our minds so that we can digest what we are listening to, rather than just hearing it.

No Judging: I can be very guilty of violating this requirement. I remember a Rotary meeting where a speaker came to present a program on a controversial issue. The issue had been voted on and passed, and now was a state law. I wasn't in favor of the legislation for strong personal reasons. As she was being introduced, I had already started "judging" the message. Here's the problem: she wasn't there to convince me it was a good law. She was simply there to raise awareness, provide resources, give data, and answer questions. She was actually a fantastic speaker. Her mission wasn't to sway minds, just to enhance knowledge. Fortunately, I was able to put my bias aside long enough to learn a few things myself. It's not always an easy thing to do.

How often in business are we "judging" someone we are listening to? It might be judging the intelligence of the person giving us advice, the motives of a sales representative, and even the purpose of someone wanting to meet with us. In order to be truly influential in our listening, we need to dispatch any preconceived notions or judgments ruminating in our minds. This is intentional and you must have some internal trigger mechanism to push you to this place when you feel that urge to pass judgment before you start "hearing" so that you can actually listen. For me, that trigger was a little voice in my head that was scratching and clawing to get through and remind me to stay unbiased. It worked for my story about the speaker at Rotary. What will your trigger mechanism be?

Slow Down: I find that my default wiring accelerates my mind when in stress-mode. I get this adrenaline rush that encourages me to do things too fast. In situations when I need to listen, yet am in this "mode," I lose full comprehension of what the other person is saying. I need to slow things down.

One of my favorite baseball players was Edgar Martínez of the Seattle Mariners. Edgar is arguably the best designated hitter (DH) in baseball history. The annual award given to best DH bears his name. I remember hearing him once, when in the prime of his career, break down the skills that made him so good. He said that when he was at his very best, it was is if the ball was coming to him in slow motion. Remember that a major league fastball can top over one hundred miles an hour at its peak. He said that the pitch slowed down to a point that he could see the stitching on the baseball. Great hitters like Edgar made it look easy because they had the ability to slow down when everything else around them was going so fast.

Think of yourself as a leader in a crisis situation. This is an area we will delve into much deeper later in this book. For now, consider the messages from multiple sources you are "hearing" when assessing the calamity. It's easy to become overwhelmed and gain nothing from these messages. You have to train your mind to slow down. This is intentional and calculated. For me, it comes from self-talk. You have to talk yourself into slowing down your heart rate, your mind, your entire countenance. You must be able to see the stitches of that ninety-nine-miles-per-hour fastball coming at you so that you can hit it out of the park. Being an influential listener requires that you listen without being rushed.

Exemplary means outstanding. The outstanding leaders in any industry or walk of life have exemplary listening skills. This doesn't have to be complex or convoluted. It really is as simple as slowing down, being in the moment, and not making judgments on the conversation or the speaker before they even start. As simple as it is, I wish I could say it was easy. However, just like in hitting a curve ball, you can practice and improve daily.

The Art & Science of Being a Raconteur
Storytelling Skills to Engage and Influence

One of my fondest childhood memories comes from my days at Olympic View Elementary in Oak Harbor, WA. Mrs. Prato was our school librarian (and my neighbor). When it came time for us to gather in the library, sit cross-legged, and listen intently, Mrs. Prato skillfully held our attention. While we may have gained much pleasure from reading the books ourselves, it never trumped being read to. The reason is because we *love* being told stories. We gather around the Thanksgiving or Christmas table and relish listening to each other's stories (at least, in our family we do). As audience members, we are more engaged when a speaker breaks into a story to help promote a message. And in actuality, our zeal for television and theater is simply for a story being "read" to us, one that's acted out in front of our very eyes.

The essence of the story you just read about Mrs. Prato is that in order to be an influential leader, you need to become a proficient storyteller. The level of sophistication in storytelling will be based on your career. However, even at the base level of being a boss, you need to exert influence and seek action on initiatives. Your skill in storytelling may just be the tipping point in understanding, commitment, and action.

There are different levels of storytelling prowess required for different careers and jobs. Here are my *3 Levels of Yarn Spinning Savvy*:

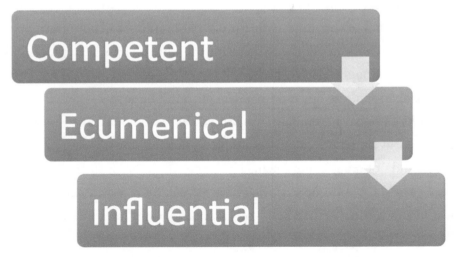

Figure 2.2

Competent: Most small businesses are run by smart people with special skills or expertise. They hire people who take the mission of the business and make it available to a target market. Elementary skills in storytelling will allow those small business owners to use a story to quickly and clearly relay instructions to their employees. They will use examples, anecdotes, and narratives for clarity and sustainability of message. Managers and supervisors in that business can do the same thing for their direct reports.

Example: A small commercial construction company is required to provide training to all employees on jobsite safety. The president or project supervisor may use personal stories as case studies to enhance the attention of the crew and more powerfully deliver an important message. It's one thing to simply tell the crew how to be safe. It's another thing to bring this message to life with a story.

Extra Point: One of my clients for my risk management consulting was a building materials dealer (e.g., lumber, windows, supplies, etc.). I was charged with giving safety training, and one of the topics was on close calls. I used a story of Captain Jack escaping out the front door with me in pursuit. I then related it to their business and how close calls need to be calls to action to avoid a future calamity. They all laughed at the story, and afterward, always asked how Captain Jack was doing. AND they remembered the message!

Ecumenical: This next level of sophistication as a speaker becomes more important for people in sales, marketing, and public relations. The ability to persuade, disclose, transmit, and build trusting relationships can be dramatically enhanced through savvy in storytelling. In fact, it's not only helpful; it's required.

Example: An insurance agent is trying to convince a prospective client to purchase life insurance. What's needed is the ability to persuade the other person through bringing them into the story, captivating their attention, and then helping them to more clearly understand the gravity or opportunity at hand.

When I was an insurance agent, selling life insurance to my business clients was part of my duties. The reason was far more serious than increased revenue or cross-selling. It was about providing the optimum value. Unfortunately, life insurance is commonly viewed as a commodity. I had a special and true story about a client who had continuously been putting off buying life insurance. He and his wife left their newborn with grandparents to take a cruise in Florida. During the cruise, one of the options for passengers was to take a charter helicopter trip into Mexico. It's one of those "cool things" that I knew my client might opt to do. Tragically, the charter helicopter crashed after leaving the cruise ship en route for Mexico. Everyone on board the helicopter was killed. When I heard the news, I knew they were on that cruise and that they might have boarded that helicopter. I panicked. I dashed on the Internet to find the news site that listed the names of the people who had perished. The wait for the old dial-tone hookup to connect was excruciating. I was happy to see that their names weren't listed. That tragic event affected them too. They bought insurance immediately on their return. This created a vivid scenario for other prospective clients about the uncertainty of life and the risk of leaving loved ones behind, penniless.

Influential: This is the highest level of storytelling, where business leaders need to be. If you're an executive, you are considered a leader not only for the employees, but also for investors, customers, shareholders, boards of directors, and the community. Political leaders must be in this category as they must be influential to earn votes. Many of them didn't start out this way, but simply by necessity transitioned here. Influential speaking does not imply bad intent. In fact, it should be focused on improving the condition of others.

Example: Steve Jobs may have been many things as the face of Apple over the decades. Regardless of your opinion of him as a business mogul, he was the epitome of the influential speaker. He had the skill to use stories to ingratiate legions of followers and a worldwide community of Apple fanatics.

I started this section by implying that storytelling is an art form. This portion of the chapter will chronicle how to turn that allegorical *ugly lump of clay* into *beautiful art*.

Art Unveiled #1—***Humor.*** You're not speaking to be Jerry Seinfeld (comedian). You are speaking to be more Will Rogers or Mark Twain. These two American legends were *humorists*. In other words, comedians use humor as the message; humorists use humor as the vehicle for the message. This is an important distinction. You don't have to consider yourself funny to uncover humor. The best way to do this when telling a story is to have humor emanate from dialogue.

Novels always have dialogue between characters. You must use the power of dialogue when telling your story. The most humorous (and important) moments occur when a final line of dialogue draws a chuckle, guffaw, or full-blown belly laugh.

While reading books on the subject of storytelling are beneficial, in order to get the most out of your talents, you need guidance and direction, either through a group like Toastmasters or a speaking coach. The next time you hear a humorist or comedian speaking, listen for dialogue and discover how it leads directly to humor.

Art Unveiled #2—***Character Development.*** Your audience wants to know whom you're talking about. Consider my Captain Jack story. I could have just said "my dog." Boring. By naming the dog (Captain Jack), describing what he looks like (Eddie from the classic sitcom *Fraser*), and giving him some personality (my Jack Russell "terrorist"), my audience can actually see him. If you're talking about your spouse, kids, pets, coworkers, or friends, you must develop their characters through:

- Names—Make them up if you must for privacy or simply give first names.
- Size and shape—We are visual people. Tall, short, slender, pudgy, glasses, hair, etc.
- Smell—Like dogs, our olfactory sense is the strongest (though not to nearly the same level). This is handy when describing cologne, perfume, or even the smell of "Granddad's" cigar.
- Demeanor—Happy, sad, excited, cautious, etc.

The best stories you read or watch all develop the characters. That's how an audience comes to have a strong emotional connection to them. Regardless of the reason for your story, it's got to be compelling. The worst thing isn't that your character is disliked because dislike is a strong emotion. The enemy of the character is apathy.

Art Unveiled #3—*Dialogue.* I referenced dialogue earlier under the "humor" section. Dialogue is crucial to being a good storyteller. It's the one place in your speaking that you can go "into character." Think about the times your parents or teachers read a book to you. When a character had dialogue, the readers would morph into that persona and speak the lines as if they were playing the part. What did that do for you? It immersed you in the story! And the good news is that we do this naturally. Listen to people telling stories in conversation. They will get animated when the dialogue part comes, even if the character isn't them.

Whether speaking to one or one thousand, being able to express your message is part of your job. Using natural dialogue and bringing a story to life separates the outstanding from the fair communicators.

Art Unveiled #4—*Vocal Variety.* The noted executive speaking coach Patricia Fripp taught me "sameness is the enemy of the speaker." Have you ever experienced a speaker who never changed his or her tone, never varied the rate of speech, and/or never altered in volume? That's called "monotonous." It's also boring.

In order to avoid this "sameness" problem, learn to improve your vocal variety. Listen on television, radio, or movies to people who have mastered this art. The variety isn't usually evident when you're not listening for it, and that's the way it's supposed to be. But if you listen carefully, you will learn that the savviest speakers vary those techniques to foster greater attentiveness.

Art Unveiled #5—*Gestures.* Gestures while telling a story lend a visible hand to your success. Gestures are meant for good, not evil. You would do well to avoid histrionics and capacious gesticulations. My technique is meant to be subtle. You can use gestures most effectively when you use them to:

- Act something out (e.g., talking on the phone)
- Signal to a location (e.g., if part of your story "took place" to your left, you can motion to there for recollection)
- Be expressive (e.g., surprise, anger, fear), yet ever so slightly. The smaller the audience the smaller the gestures. If you're speaking to a large audience, then you must be bigger than you had even imagined to ensure that even the person in the back row sees you.
- Be different. Remember that sameness is the enemy of speakers. Talking without a single movement is unnatural and awkward after about five minutes.

Final thought: Language has and always will be the major factor in creating and developing relationships, both professionally and personally. You can't turn this talent on and off like a faucet. It's a skill that needs to be honed daily in order to be your default. The better you become, the more influential and persuasive you will be, thus making your success in maximizing your skills and talents more likely.

Wicked Vocabulary

I may be a dog, but I have a wicked vocabulary. Just because humans don't hear words, doesn't mean that we dogs aren't always clear on our intent.

Dan talks about being in the moment. That's a crazy concept to me because we dogs never stress about the past or worry about the future. We are always in the moment. My vocabulary is based on smell. That's right, smell. You humans use your vision; we use our olfactory sense to figure out things. That's how we know if there is danger or opportunity. It's also how we know if some other dog marked our spot!

When I'm testy, I have a certain bark. If I'm hungry, the bark is completely different. When I want to play, everyone knows it just through my body language. Humans are the same. You use words and visual cues to communicate. Too bad you don't always know what you want, or you make assumptions about what others want. Take it from me, it's best to be clear about you and let the other person be clear about themselves. If you don't have a wicked vocabulary like I do, you can end up barking up the wrong tree if you're not careful! Don't let that happen to you!

Just saying. . .

Captain Jack

Playing for Each Other

CREATING AN UNLEASHED CULTURE

I never smoke to excess—that is, I smoke in moderation,
only one cigar at a time.

~ **Mark Twain**

Like the legendary humorist Mark Twain, I also smoke in "moderation." Normally, I leave it to special occasions, or at least monthly, when I'm simply relaxing and enjoying life. One such occasion was in spring 2014 when I was sitting poolside at the home of my professional mentor, Alan Weiss. Alan has a beautiful house in Rhode Island that overlooks a private lake filled with birds, frogs, and other wildlife. My colleagues and I sat poolside observing the dogs playing on the grounds and watching an occasional fish pop up through the smooth water.

As I sat smoking a rich and piquant cigar, a new observation dawned on me. In order to light up and enjoy the corona, three components are all necessary. The requirements are heat, fuel, and oxygen. Without each of these three elements, the cigar won't even light. The triumvirate of combustible fuel (the rolled tobacco), ignited by adequate heat (flame), and sustained by oxygen (the air) created a burning cigar. All organically found and leveraged, these three constituents need each other to result in enjoyment for the stogie aficionado.

The same is true for the mindset of *playing for each other*. It's easy to go to work and simply trade time for money, to earn a paycheck and go home. It's quite another thing to be part of a team that cares and works for the benefit of each member. The best athletic teams "buy in" to the notion of playing for their teammates. This idea not only works on the athletic field or court, it works in boardrooms, offices, and manufacturing plants too. And it's easier said than done!

In this chapter, we will discuss concepts, topics, and best practices around creating a culture of "we" in your company. We will do that by introducing critical team building concepts that sports teams have used successfully for decades. We begin by seeing what my cigar and your company have in common!

My cigar needed this in order to light and stay burning:

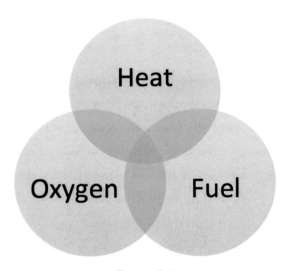

Figure 3.1

Without each component doing its job, a flame won't even start. After ignition, without the constant inclusion of these elements, the flame will burn out quickly and quietly. Now that's sad. . .

Let's transfer the concept to your business and its culture. You also need three elements to ignite the flame of your organization. They are Diversity, Desirability, and Reward. Here is the second visual that represents this concept:

Figure 3.2

Just like the flame, all three components are required for a healthy, balanced, and growing company. If I want to finish my cigar and maximize my enjoyment, I need to keep that bad boy burning. If you want to unleash your skills to help your clients (and your business) improve, you will need to do the same.

Dealing With Diversity
How to Get Everyone to Play Nice in the Sandbox

Diversity comes wrapped in many "boxes." These gifts might include a number of themes:

- Generations in the workplace
- Gender diversity
- Outside experiences from other organizations
- Cultures and races
- Skill sets and social styles
- Communication and learning styles
- Habits and outlooks on life

My daughter Kelli works for Nordstrom as a marketing planner in their corporate office in Seattle. When she got the job, she learned that for years this fabled and highly successful company almost exclusively hired from within. People would start their careers on the retail floor selling clothes and shoes, and then eventually be hired into roles with greater responsibility that would lead to the corporate suites. To the credit of the company, employees were loyal and stayed an amazingly long time. However, as the company continued to grow and become more visionary in its brands and marketing, the leadership knew they needed fresh viewpoints and ideas. They understood that if you only breathe your own exhaust, you are in grave danger of asphyxiation.

Kelli is an ideal example of this paradigm shift. Her background in school was as a business major with an emphasis in sports management. She spent three years working for the Pittsburgh Marathon. This race brings in over thirty-two thousand runners from across the world, and her role was to work with elite athletes and market the event on social media and other major platforms. That experience helped her earn her job at Nordstrom as an "outsider." That's because they made a commitment to diversifying their thinking and not breathing their own exhaust.

Diversity in thinking is only one paradigm shift. As a leader, you need to seek out other diversities. Here are four case studies for you to ruminate over:

1. **Gender**—Even though we find ourselves well into the twenty-first century, there is still work to be done in gender equity in pay. The good news is that more women are being considered for and given opportunities. The work needs to (and I am certain, will) continue. When I was on the school board, at one point all five board spots were occupied by men. We had little control over this situation, as it was an elected position. That being said, a school board made up of all middle-aged white men can be very astigmatic, which isn't good for the school district or even for board relations. That got reversed at the next election to the

betterment of the organization and constituency. You may have little control over this depending on your role in your company. However, influence in building gender diversity is important, and NOT simply because of having a female body in place. It's the variety and perspective that offers value to the company and the customers.

2. **Race**—Race diversity can't be viewed as an obligation or item to be marked off a checklist. It must be real. While there are organizations (like the National Football League) that require the interviewing of minority groups, that is a more difficult concept to carry through to small business. Diversity in race brings fresh viewpoints and perspectives and should be considered as a benefit. That being said, the candidate for employment must have the skill sets and should be hired on merit first.

3. **Generations**—This book isn't going to delve deeply into this issue. There are entire books just for that purpose. However, it is a reality that five generations can actually work together in the same company. That brings a level of complexity for the human resources manager, yet a wide net of opportunity for the company. More on this shortly.

4. **Outsiders**—*Outsiders* are easily viewed as a threat internally. While you might think that this isn't really diversity, let's be clear that it is. New ideas brought in from outside the organization are often viewed with skepticism and fear. Fear that change might not work, and fear that it might.

In the end, what matters is not so much the *type* of diversity you have in your company, but how you use it. Unleashed leaders don't simply celebrate assessments about having diversity in numbers. Unleashed leaders maximize the strength of the pack. To be a leader who drives results through maximum performance means that you need to ensure that all members of the team are leaving no talent on the table. Here are five easy steps to ensure that:

1. **Seek out qualified and diverse applicants**. You don't need to have a specific rule in effect to be cognizant of great talent that comes in different packages. If you find yourself lacking a diverse company culture, be on the lookout for how you can make changes, even if they're internal.

2. **Encourage ideas.** Make sure everyone in the organization knows that ideas are welcome from everyone. This can't be assumed; a leader in the different situations that present themselves must manage it.

3. **Set them up for success.** Later in this book we will go into greater detail on organizational coaching, mentoring, and accountability programs. For now, suffice it to say that providing adequate training is imperative.

4. **Deal swiftly with conflict.** Conflict can either be healthy or unhealthy for your company. It's sometimes not even very clear which is which, yet you only want the former. This is where developing a strong management team is paramount for success. You can't allow any issues or drama to fester.

5. **Be consistent.** The worst thing you can do as a leader is be inconsistent. That being said, sometimes being consistent needs to be defined. As a girls' high school basketball coach, I worked tirelessly my first few years to be "consistent" in how I treated and responded to players. I never wanted there to be any implication of favorites. In fact, some of the better players may have borne the brunt of overcompensation at times!

   During my fifth year of coaching, one of the best pieces of advice I received from one of my coaching mentors, was this: You can't treat everyone the same because people respond differently. The rules are all the same; however, how you engage with individuals may be just as different as they are.

   Bruce said, "Dan, respond to your players the opposite to how their fathers do [and believe me, we knew how their fathers behaved!]. If the father is really loud and obnoxious, be patient and subtle. If the father is low-key and unobtrusive, you can be more direct and tough." Turns out, he was right. The players on my team responded much better to me when I kept this tenet in mind. In fact, to my surprise, nobody ever complained about inequality.

Generations

It would be remiss of me to not discuss the hot topic of generations in the workplace and how a leader can make this a positive rather than a negative. I have yet to work with any clients who haven't had to deal with an issue related to generations in their workplace, or who haven't wanted to know how to improve their leadership in this area.

I look at it from a central viewpoint. I don't want to put people or generations in a box. We are a product more of our surroundings and our environments than the generation we were born into. All that said, I have respect for my colleagues who work in this area and have come to accept many of their theses. Here is my favorite. . .

A colleague named Anna Liotta is an expert in the field of generations. She has written books and spoken on it nationally. One day, while at lunch, she shared an intriguing theory on the compatibility of generations. She said that generations that lived through the same experiences, adversity, challenges, and prosperity around the age of ten would have a similar "generational view."

Example: People born in 1931 and 1991 in the United States will have a comparable worldview. You see, when these folks were ten years old (give or take), a very significant and homogeneous event happened. In 1941, Japan attacked Pearl Harbor causing widespread fear, anger, and profound sadness. In 2001, the same feelings materialized for ten-year-olds when the Twin Towers in New York City were the focus of the September 11 terror attacks. Both events led to war (World War II and the War on Terror), followed by economic prosperity. Those events shaped kids of a same age in the same way, and according to Anna, makes these two generations compatible when communicating and working together.

I have three basic rules for my clients in dealing with generations, especially the youngest and newest entering the workplace. It's not uncommon for me to hear complaints about the *Millennials* being lazy, selfish, entitled, and plugged into all of their technology to the detriment of their brains and all those around them. My experience is that there are plenty of more "mature" adults that resemble these adjectives. We need to focus more on people than generations. With that in mind, here are my rules for improving your leadership when it comes to generations:

1. **Stop Judging and Start Learning.** The same judgments about the *Millennial* generation are the same complaints every generation has fostered for the most current. Words and phrases like *lazy, entitled, self-absorbed, moody,* and *poor communication skills* are pervasive. I do workshops around the country where this topic is raised, and these generalizations always bubble to the surface. Here is the reality: young people today live in a very different world than we did. They grew up with technology and use it for communications, making reservations, playing games, and lodging complaints all over the social media landscape. That doesn't make them any of the words previously mentioned. It means they are just the beginning of the cyber revolution that will include more employees and all of your customers, clients, and prospects of the future. You might just want to learn how they do what they do, and how they can most benefit you and your company in its growth.

2. **It's Not Your Way or the Highway Anymore.** Remember when a boss could simply say, "Hey, it's my way, or you can look for another job down the highway. . .?" Back then, they were much closer to right than they are today. Young people have many more options to make money and don't need you as much as you need them. That's exactly why recruiting and hiring has

become such a major issue. Young people are experts at seeking new opportunities and usually aren't willing to give you every opportunity to show them you care. It's incumbent on you to do a good job of welcoming them to your organization (as you should everyone) and providing them with the tools to advance quickly. If you don't, you will ultimately be adversely selected against. That means the fair to poor employees stay, and the great ones find new pastures.

3. **Give Them More Responsibility, Not Less.** Base their roles and responsibilities on observed behavior and results, not time on the job. Public school districts are often hampered by agreements where teachers are more valued for tenure rather than performance. A mediocre teacher can last long enough to never get fired, yet a bright new teacher can be terminated because of budget cuts. Businesses can (and do) get caught up in the same mentality by just thinking that members of a younger generation need to earn their stripes, get their noses and knees bloodied a little, and pay their dues. That's the type of thinking that holds organizations back and keeps them from reaching their optimum results.

The Holy Grail
*Recruiting and Hiring Strategies and
Techniques to Hire and Reward the Right People*

My clients often tell me that recruiting and hiring good people is the "Holy Grail" of their business. They spend a large chunk of their time on activities that lead to hiring strong people. The problem is that they often get bogged down using the wrong "carrot." The prize at the end of the stick needs to be more than financially based. That carrot needs to be one that offers a sense of *reward* as a significant part of the equation.

If you're familiar with Daniel Pink's book *Drive: The Surprising Truth about What Motivates Us*, then you will recall his theory that money isn't the sole factor in recruiting, hiring, and keeping (emphasis on the latter) good people. Mr. Pink believes that factors dealing with non-financial rewards (at least when the income is fair and a level of comfort in lifestyle is achieved) are most important when motivating, inspiring, and retaining the very best and brightest employees. The very best people you hire are most likely the ones that are most open to trying new things, learning from you, and ameliorating the culture in your organization. They are most likely to be Unleashed.

I made my first professional mark in the world in the insurance industry. Right after college, I was hired as an underwriter by United Pacific Insurance outside of Seattle. After a year and a half, it became clear to me that sitting in a cubicle all day long and deciding who deserved auto insurance was not the career for me. Apparently, my personality was evident to one of my agency clients, and they recruited me to become an agent. That became my first foray into the world of sales.

Bell-Anderson Insurance was a fine agency that specialized in all lines of insurance. Although I was originally hired as a personal insurance agent, I quickly transitioned into selling commercial (business) insurance. I found it to be more *rewarding*. While it certainly offered the ability to earn higher income; just as importantly, it kept me from being bored! It was a constant challenge because of the diversity of clients and prospects I would work with. Almost no client would be the same, and I needed that challenge, whether I understood it at the time or not.

The sales team (called "producers") met twice a month on the first and third Mondays. At the first meeting of the month, we would review sales for the previous month. Our agency president, Steve, would bring a freshly minted, nearly flawless one hundred dollar bill for the producer who had the highest sales for that previous month. Steve would take that crisp, clean Benjamin Franklin and present it to the recipient at the meeting. I was fortunate enough to, on occasion, merit that prize.

Let's be clear about one thing regarding this reward. While one hundred dollars is nothing to sneeze at, this was not a financial bonus. If you know much about the psychology of sales people, you will observe that *recognition* is a reward that is greatly desired. For successful producers, the one hundred dollars was meager compared to the regular commissions they were earning. Had Steve simply added it to the month's salary draw, nobody would have given it much thought. However, when he made a big deal of the presentation of that currency, then all of a sudden, it became a motivation to all of us. Sounds silly. However, the motivating factor was real and rampant among the most successful producers.

I just listed two motivations outside of money that were predominant for me personally in my time at Bell-Anderson. The first was *challenge*, and the second was *recognition*. The people you are trying to recruit, hire, and keep want to know more than just how much money you can throw at them. It's your job to figure out what those rewards are. Let's break it down for each of these three components. . .

Recruiting

1. **Create a value proposition for your company.** I don't mean a mission statement; I mean a value proposition. What is it that you as an organization do to improve the condition of your clients/customers? How about of your employees? The value proposition might be something like, "We ensure the protection of our client's lifestyle for as long as they live." People working in your company need to know that they are working for the good of something other than your revenue. They must feel that someone is benefiting from their work.

2. **Use outcome-based language when recruiting.** I've held workshops where I've asked participants what value they bring to employees. To a person, they spouted generic bromides such as "We offer a great benefit package," or "We offer comprehensive training," or "We have flexible hours for our workers." Bottom line, these are all *things*, rather than *outcomes*.

Change your language to "You will find a benefit package that is flexible for your personal or family needs so you can get exactly what you need." And "Your professional development will be advanced quickly through our internal training program so that you can avoid the obstacles to maximizing your talent." And "You will find our flexible hours program of benefit because you can now create a work schedule that allows you to best conform to your family's situation." Notice they all say basically the same thing; however, the latter examples personalize the value to the recruit. It's about them, not everyone.

3. **Recruit people, not positions.** I have a very good client who taught me this concept. Mike runs an insurance company that has a national marketing concentration on a specific line of professional insurance for architects and engineers. Mike has about fifty employees working for him in various roles from sales to marketing to customer service. Mike told me that he never hires specifically looking to fill a position. He thinks that desperation can creep in and result in poor hires. He focuses on constantly recruiting smart people and determining how their talents and skills fit into his company. You will read more about how Mike makes this system really successful in a few paragraphs. Mike has a company filled with outstanding people that are all unleashing their talents in the right roles because they were hired for their singularity as people, rather than because they were warm bodies.

Hiring

1. **Onboard ingenuity.** One of the traps that small business owners often fall into is that upon hiring someone new, they have no formal plan for bringing them "onboard" effectively. While the larger companies normally have some system, even that can be convoluted and confusing. If you want to get someone Un-

leashed into their roles quickly, have a plan to get them there. This includes all the human resources paperwork (now most often forced through technology, which from what I've seen, can be more laborious and confounding), the proper introduction to team members and coworkers, any help with procuring log-in credentials and other job-related resources, and an introduction to their mentor (next step. . .stay tuned). These "onboarding" techniques must be done at the outset, must be clear, and must put these folks into a position of comfort, not fear and apprehension.

2. **Mentor.** When I went to work at United Pacific in 1987, I was given a mentor. When I arrived at Bell-Anderson less than two years later, I was given a pen, a pad of paper, a rate book, and a barren desk. This isn't to be judgmental of the agency; it's just a fact that small businesses are more apt to eschew any type of formal mentoring because they feel they lack time and manpower. They don't. It's just a matter of making it a priority. Mentoring can be done in even the smallest of offices. The best thing about mentoring is that (if done well) you can set the stage for the culture of *playing for each other*. On sports teams, these mentors are often the older players that have "been there and done that." They take on these roles in the locker room, usually on a more informal basis. However, it's part of the culture. In your company, it needs to be more thoughtful and intentional.

3. **Give it thirty days.** People are becoming savvier about getting hired. They understand how keywords are used on online applications. They are able to get in the door and normally say things and pass tests based on acumen around getting hired, rather than being the right fit. Based on what clients have told me, you get a pretty good read on someone after thirty days. It's somewhat like dating—the beginning is that romantic "getting to know you" stage. After thirty days, the real person will always

emerge. As part of the original hire, you need to be cognizant of red flags that a person might not be the right fit for your company. In addition, you also need to be open to the fact that while they may be the right type of person for your organization, their skills may match another role or responsibility better. More on this in the next section.

Keeping

1. **Develop your bench strength.** Earlier you read about my client, Mike. He hires people, not positions. He then trains people in all relevant jobs in the organization. They take some time to work and understand all the roles. This practice serves dual purposes. First, Mike learns what the best strengths and talents are in each person. Maybe they were slotted for certain roles, but after watching them perform, he realizes that they fit better in different ones. Second, he develops "bench strength." No matter the success or culture of a company, people will come and go. On occasion, you need to pull someone internally to help out where needed. This is bench strength, and it helps you avoid the dilemma of hiring for positions.

2. **Mentor and coach (redux).** Here's the deal: mentoring and coaching work. Whether you're aiding the development of your talented assets internally or externally, it matters not. What is critical is that your new hires continue to develop, grow, and deal with issues throughout the first eighteen months of employment. That's the break-even point on your return on investment, and a marker that this person is more likely to be a long-time employee doing good work for you and maximizing their talent. Leadership isn't just doing the coaching; it's being smart enough to know it's needed and provide that access.

Extra Point: Often people think of leaders in the same vein as "teachers." Actually, coaching and mentoring should often be done by others, either from within the organization or hired in. I've worked as a coach for many CEOs and presidents of organizations. I've also been hired by them to work with their key management. In other cases, I've been hired to train organizations on how to be good mentors. In fact, some of my best clients have been several Department of Defense installations. They understand the concept of professional development and how mentors and coaches play a role. You should too.

3. **Set metrics for success.** Alan Weiss often refers to setting metrics by using the phrase, "How would you know if you tripped over it?" Having physically tripped over many an item in my life, I agree with this allegory!

   The best way to assess your success in hiring new people and your recruitment and hiring process is to keep tabs on it. Whatever role this new person is playing—sales, customer service, technology, or human resources—there are measures that you set. They may be unique to you, or perhaps measures set as benchmarks in associations you belong to. Whatever they are, set them and then be diligent. At a later point in this book, we will discuss my concept of *gravitational pull*. Setting solid metrics—both qualitative and quantitative—will aid in avoiding this malady.

Do You Taste Like Chicken?
Devising Desirability for Your Business

Sameness.

The noted executive speech coach Patricia Fripp has surmised that *sameness* is the enemy of the speaker. It's the killer for businesses when it comes to marketing their products *and* services and seeking talent.

Several years ago, I attended a wild game dinner fundraiser replete with exotic hors d'oeuvres featuring animals that I was most familiar watching roam the prairies and jungles on the old American television series *Wild Kingdom*. They served antelope, wild boar, alligator, and cougar. The one thing that I most remember from the experience was hearing the servers proclaim about almost every offering, *"Don't worry. . .it tastes like chicken."*

That adage has become a part of our culture, whether you're describing water buffalo, kangaroo, or cane toads. Chicken has become the generic standard that we base all other meats on. If it tastes like chicken, we are "safe."

Here's the problem. If everything tastes like chicken, it loses that joy of adventure and curiosity. It becomes stale and uninteresting. It's just chicken.

The very same problem can happen to you and your business. If your customers and target market consider you to *taste like chicken,* then you've sunk into the abyss of ordinary and generic. You're boring. When that happens, your viability is as threatened as a chubby chicken wandering aimlessly in a poultry farm. *Dead meat walking.*

Tasting like chicken can be poisonous to the desirability of your company to both current and potential employees alike. How do you know if you "taste like chicken"? Why don't we cross that road by considering these signs?

1. **Your employees can't verbalize your organizational value.**
   In other words, what makes you special? Why would someone work with you, rather than a competitor? How do you improve the condition and lives of others based on your unique value? Do you simply spout out the old, tired "We have great customer service" as an answer? Meh. . .

2. **Your website is outdated.** Believe me, all generations will judge your sophistication based on the quality of your website. Boring website equates to boring employer.

3. **You do the same thing as everyone else.** Go back and reread #1. If you can't recount why you're different, you will become

white noise. If you're comfortable being "competitive" rather than being bold, then you taste like flavorless chicken.

4. **You lack team building.** I'm not implying any touchy-feely exercise replete with walking on scorching hot coals or catching an employee falling from a twenty-foot drop. The Unleashed companies create opportunities to engage, collaborate, and build a sense of family.

5. **You lack diversity.** Hmm, where have I seen this before? Lack of diversity in thinking equals boring. . .again.

If any of these signs pervade your company or you, then you're probably beginning to smell like the chicken dinner that is served up at your low-budget banquet event. Here are three quick strategies and tactics that you can implement immediately to mix up the menu, bringing new flavors and adding spice to your world and to your team:

1. **Create an organizational value proposition.** Remember this concept was introduced earlier in this chapter? Don't wave your well-worn and mindlessly memorized mission statement at me. You need to have a team that knows the value you bring to your clients and customers. They need to be able to spread that results-oriented message to anyone within the sound of their voice (or a corresponding computer monitor). Not an elevator speech, rather, a pithy and powerful statement of what your company is good at and how you manifest it to the world.

   Case Study: The Disney Corporation makes a statement about what they offer their customers. Note that I didn't say "board of directors" or "shareholders." Their customers. . .just like you and me. For as long as I can remember, the parks were promoted as "The Happiest Place on Earth!" How can you beat that? The value statement is that you go there and you will be happy beyond your wildest expectations. Can you so succinctly and effectively illustrate your value? Can your employees?

   The Fix: Put your feet up on your desk, clasp your hands behind your head and think. That's right, think. What are you good at. . . really good at? What has made you successful and why? I've found that querying clients and customers and lifting sound bites from their responses is one of the best ways to discover your value. If they've been the recipients of remarkable value, they can explain it even more eloquently than you can. Sometimes the most valuable work you will do as a leader is to stop, think, and ask questions. Keep it simple.

2. **Change your look.** If you look, act, and smell like a chicken, well, then you're a chicken. Many business owners are scared of looking different in fear of being viewed as silly. Instead, they need to be unique.

   Case Study: Steve Jobs never settled for being identical to any of his competitors. The Apple mogul bucked conventionality by being obsessive about how his product looked when delivered. While most PC providers shipped out their equipment in monolithic boxes that took a degree in physics to unwrap, Jobs was preoccupied with making the actual box not only user-friendly, but also fun and cool. He believed that the customers should have joy, excitement, and fun when receiving their new product, and that packaging was the first step in that process. It's like a discerning doorman welcoming you to a five-star hotel.

   The Fix: Be willing to be nimble. Be willing to change, even if it goes against the norm. Spend time strategizing, being contrarian, and determining what is best for your customers and your team. When your employees believe they are part of something unique, this builds trust and loyalty. And you might just find it brings in new ideas!

3. **Don't fix your own swing.** As an avid golfer, I often think I can fix my swing when things go awry. Sometimes I can. Sometimes I can't, and I waste a lot of energy. Business and companies can get into a rut as bad as my golf game can. I've

heard many entrepreneurs firmly assert that they can fix their swing when things go bad. When it comes to recruiting and hiring, sometimes you just need to get out of your own way and get help. Sophisticated golfers do it. . . so can you. Here's what I mean: You might become myopic in how you seek (or maybe don't seek) new blood. There's nothing wrong with hiring experts. Sometimes, they might be the ones who do the work for you, or they might be the consultants you need to help you do it. Hiring has become more treacherous over the past two decades. There are things you can and cannot say. There are rules and regulations that you have to stay current on. Too many people get into a lot of trouble when they don't know what they are doing in the recruiting and hiring process. Recruiting and hiring really strong talent—the Holy Grail—isn't something you need to do on your own. Get help to ensure that your system in this process is as flawless as a Jack Nicklaus swing.

Bottom line: **If you are perceived to be chicken, your goose is cooked.** The business world demands difference and innovation, speed and accessibility, and technological sophistication and savvy. *Your potential employees* demand difference. Recruits and potential team members will demand diversity in people and products, out-of-the-box thinking when it comes to compensation and rewards, and a culture that is about playing for each other, not just a paycheck. Does your business taste like chicken? If it does, don't despair. You can always change the menu as long as you have the courage to do so.

Are you hungry?

Championship Building
How to Sustain an Organizational Culture

Professional sports used to be dominated by legendary dynasties—the Green Bay Packers, Boston Celtics, and New York Yankees quickly come to mind. These teams were THE dynasties for multiple generations, starting back as early as the 1920s. Free agency and a tremendous push for parity in all professional leagues has made it virtually impossible for any franchise to do that again. The closest probably have been the New England Patriots of the National Football League and the St. Louis Cardinals in Major League Baseball over the past decade. Even then, their runs have never equaled the storied success of their predecessors.

The biggest challenge to sports franchises carrying greatness for season after season is pretty simple. Churn. Every year, there is significant churn in the organization with players coming and going, based not on ability or desire to keep them, but salary cap and free agency. It has made parity a reality, which is good for sports. It's not what you want for your business, though.

The legendary business guru Peter Drucker once quipped, "Culture eats strategy for breakfast." Culture is in every organization. It's one of three things: Good, Bad, or Indifferent. Only good is good. . .how's that for being deep? We've spent some time in this chapter talking about creating a culture of "playing for each other." We discussed how to recruit, hire, keep, and create diversity. Now, how do we set a mindset of "playing for each other?" And once we have it, how do we sustain it? Let's talk about this now. . .

Contrary to popular sayings, I don't believe that most humans are only in this for themselves. I believe we enjoy being like unleashed dogs—pack animals working for the welfare of every member of the pack. Rudyard Kipling once stated that "the strength of the Pack is the Wolf, and the strength of the Wolf is the Pack." He was correct about both wolves and humans.

While some of you out there might be lone wolves, you undoubtedly need the help of others to succeed. I can attest to this as a solo practitioner consultant. I may not have employees, but my "pack" includes my accountant, attorney, web designer, mentor, accountability partner, banker, and technology guru, to name a few. If you're running, managing, or owning a business, your pack is far more substantial. If you're leading the pack, you'd better know in which direction you're headed and who has your back.

Playing for each other means caring why you're doing your work, not just that you are doing it. You might be an expert in your field and perform your job well; however, if your end result is getting it done, cashing your paycheck, and cruising towards retirement, you will never reach your full potential. Neither for that matter, will your company. As a leader, you must instill the "playing for each other" mindset.

Extra Point: My hometown NFL team is the Seattle Seahawks. In the 2014 season, the concept of "playing for your teammates" became a battle cry for the defending Super Bowl champions. They had become distracted by all the folderol and hoopla associated with winning a Super Bowl. In fact, it's clear that some selfishness had crept into the "working ranks," namely the locker room. Head Coach Pete Carroll called together the team leaders, and they collectively brought the team back together for an airing of grievances. It worked, and they were a different team from then on. While they didn't repeat as champions, they returned to the Super Bowl, which is a feat that had last been done a decade before. Pete Carroll showed tremendous leadership. Leadership in the face of adversity is one thing. Getting everyone back on the same page to act as a team is another.

Business isn't unlike football when creating a mindset and culture of putting your coworkers needs in front of your own. While your team may not be concerning themselves with physical blocking, tackling, and scoring touchdowns, you do have your own versions of these. For your consideration:

- Customer service actively seeking referrals for sales staff to help them sell new business.
- Sales staff intentionally completing all their paperwork to make life easier on service.
- Human resources staff proactively working to allay gossip and drama to keep any distractions away from management.
- Management being cognizant to rewarding staff for work being

done well, in an effort to recognize others for their efforts.

- Coworkers confronting the poor behavior of others. This is important. Playing for each other doesn't imply constant harmony. There are times in every business and every family where people might need to be called out for the betterment of each other and the organization. I work with clients in the construction industry. Many of the jobs and projects involve a higher than normal level of danger. Not keeping others accountable can cause them or someone else getting hurt, as well as reputation damage to the company. You know you have a strong culture when your team polices itself successfully.

- Employees picking up the work of others without complaint when someone is sick, on vacation, or just in need of help.

So here is an exercise for you to jump-start your business (or at least the team you manage). . .

Unleashed Exercise: Identify at least ten ways in which your team can display "playing for each other." I gave you some ideas to help you, but I want you to create your own. Don't self-edit. You're brainstorming. The next step is to turn this into an exercise for your entire team. Ask them to do the same thing and then discuss. The conversation should be about how each person can enhance the practice for the betterment of the team. I've done this with groups, and even at a basic level, it works.

A culture of "playing for each other" sounds great and often builds up strong initial momentum. Unfortunately, there are often obstacles that will get in the way. Outside factors like time burdens, distractions, drama, and other crises can waylay your best-laid and developed plans. Selfishness and vanity can also be factors, especially after big success (reflect on my Extra Points story about the Seahawks). Here is my **5-point Strategy for Sustain-**

ing a *Play for Each Other* **Culture**:

Point 1—Make It a Priority for You. If it's not a priority for you, it's a priority for nobody. It's easy to gloss over this and say it's a given. However, you will be subject to the same distractions. Your actions and accountability to the changes implemented and the behaviors desired will be the foundation for their success.

Point 2—Make Your Leaders Accountable. Sports teams with strong leadership police themselves. Team leaders are often heard repeating the mission and vision given by coaches, and more importantly, they genuinely believe it. Your leaders may be your direct reports, your managers/supervisors, or in the case of a family business, your brother or sister. The priority and accountability starts with you and is manifested in your organizational leadership team.

Point 3—Brutal Candor Required. You know that communication is critical to any business or personal success. There is no place for egos or hurt feelings. Lines of communication must be honest and expeditious. Focus on observed behaviors and make corrections when needed. Professionalism is a necessity, yet it's critical to be able to provide open and straightforward criticism and solutions without negative repercussions.

Point 4—Speed Is King. Act rapidly on issues that become obstacles to momentum and growth. The longer you wait and the more you procrastinate, the harder it will be. I believe that employees desire good working situations. Disagreements and professional conflict are fine. Drama, gossip, and manipulative behavior are not. Be able to quickly identify problems and course correct with the nimbleness of a speedboat.

Point 5—Be Patient. I've found in our virtual, need-it-now business climate, patience is often lacking, or at least, in very short supply. Behavioral and organizational culture change requires patience from the Unleashed leader. You should be open and forthcoming with praise and rewards for what you want, and patient and coaching when people fall short of the mark. There will always be slips and declines. The important issue is that morale never dips so low that you have to climb that big hill again. Combating obstacles is comparable to watching a good stock trend up regardless of the slight pullbacks. You are seeking success, not perfection.

Sirius Smoke

Dan smokes a cigar once a month. Barb makes him go out on the back deck so the smoke doesn't stay in the house. She will normally join him out there, unless it's really cold. I go with him regardless of the conditions. Why? There's something about hanging out as guys and smelling the sweet smell of the cigar waft into the air that comforts me. That, and he will normally bring out a few things to nibble on and the chance of picking up crumbs is very high!

Dan smokes a cigar for pleasure and enjoyment. I chase my tail for the same reason. I've noted that many humans spend an inordinate amount of time being anxious, unhappy, troubled, and downright despondent. I have a theory.

Dan has picked up from me that life is supposed to be fun. Not everything that happens in life is fun, but the overall attitude about life should be. When you never allow yourself time to relax and recharge, you're doomed for burn out. It's like a cigar getting snuffed out before you even get to the band! That's leaving money on the table if you ask me.

We dogs love rewards. Bella and I get treats when we do things well (or when Dan needs to get us out of a room). We love to rejuvenate with naps and television watching (at least, I do). Dan says you have to plan relaxation into your life, even schedule it. I don't understand that, but hey, if it's the only way humans can manage their priorities, so be it.

The fastest way to smother your flame (i.e., zest for life) is to stamp out the oxygen. When Dan finally finishes his cigar, he literally removes the oxygen. When humans (because you will never find dogs doing this) extinguish their inspiration, then they never achieve all that they could have. Take a cue from us dogs and my cigar-smoking pal, take some time out to reward, relax, and recharge, even if you have to force yourself to do it. That's best way to keep the fire burning.

Just saying. . .
Captain Jack

Whom Do You Play For?

HOW TO ENSURE A WINNING TEAM

Do you remember choosing teams to play games as a kid? My sports of choice were baseball, basketball, and football. Two captains would be "anointed" depending on the social structure of the playground. In my experience, they were normally the two best players, and their leadership roles had nothing to do with their ability to lead the teams or even pick good players. The remaining athletes would be lined up opposite the captains, staring intently at them, trying to be the next person selected. The ultimate humiliation was being in the final two, knowing only one would be the ignominious last pick.

If you're familiar with the AMC hit television show *Mad Men*, you may recall, at the end of the third season, advertising executive Don Draper recruits a group of people to leave the firm, including two partners, and form their own agency. They took drastic and covert action when they found out that their old agency was being sold and they didn't want to play along. At the conclusion of the episode, which is the season finale, you see Draper standing in the hotel room that is temporarily being used as the new office. He is gazing at the small group of people he handpicked to "play ball" with the new agency. These were the people he personally chose to move forward with. He had "picked his team."

In 2008, as I was preparing to take the presidency of my Rotary Club, one of the guest speakers in the workshop I was attending asked a compelling question. He queried, "If your club had to whittle itself down to only twenty-five members, would you be one of them?" This was a poignant question for me as I was in a large club of one hundred thirty members.

If you had to choose five people to move forward in building a new organization, whom would you choose? Why? Would you even be one of them? And as the boss, what would your leadership style be?

Does your style encourage or discourage prosperity and significance? Are you providing leadership with passion, skill, and inspiration? Would your employees or your "team" trade you for someone else? Are you enhancing or detracting from your organization's performance? *How do you know?* Honest evaluation needs to be done on the entire team, including you.

Whom would you go to battle with if you only had four other people to choose? What characteristics make them your choice? What role do you play in best igniting their talent? Let's tackle those questions and more right now.

Picking Teams

My playground experiences as a youth might be different from yours, as we all come from different backgrounds, experiences, and of course, playgrounds. In my personal experience, competition and the desire to win those schoolyard contests always trumped popularity. On our playground, you were most popular when you delivered the best results.

When I became an adult and went into the workforce, I noted that wasn't always the practice. Many of you might have had experiences where players were chosen by teams based on popularity over results. In some organizations, you might find employees commonly being vetted based on non-results, like being pleasant or cheerful. One of the phrases I hear when discussing employee issues with clients is ". . .and they are *so nice.*" Team members are often promoted and chosen for new roles based on their seniority. In too many cases, they can't even be let go because of the length of tenure. In my *Mad Men* example above, Don Draper didn't care about personality as much as he cared about competence, talent, and results.

What about you? What do you look for in your ideal team members?

The following list is one that is carved out of the old playground unwritten rules, where egos were left in the classroom and all that mattered was having fun and winning. You can use this "Top 10" as a guide to helping you identify issues and lead your team:

1. **Can they play?** Skill comes right to the top of the pile when determining fit. While the following factors are also important, skill is a given. Does your "player" have the raw talent, the skill, and the ability to improve and get better?

2. **Are they coachable?** On the playground, the captain will often assign positions, roles, and responsibilities. Can your player adapt? Are they versatile? Are they willing to learn and be coached? Everyone says they are "coachable" in the interview stage. You will see how honest they are somewhere in the first thirty to forty-five days.

3. **Do they have grit?** When I coach and mentor insurance sales professionals, I remind them that they are in the *rejection business.* The ability to take a punch, to be resilient when rejected, and to get up and try again with a smile on your face is required in business. Grit is about emotional toughness.

4. **Will they speak up?** Nobody wants a "yes man." Maybe the most meaningful characteristic trait for team members is the confidence to professionally voice their opinion and dissent. These people are invaluable watchdogs and barometers to decision-making.

5. **Do they play well with others?** You need happy, positive people on your team. I'm not talking about insincere people who have ulterior motives (remember the Eddie Haskell character from the old *Leave It To Beaver* television series?). They get found out quickly. You spend a majority of your time with

coworkers, not your family. Work can be challenging enough. Surround yourself with people whom you want around you.

6. **Are they interesting?** You may be curious about this one. Here's the deal: you want people on your team who are interesting because they provide diversity and knowledge. Seek out people who read books of all genres, who travel, who have unique hobbies, who have world experiences, and who offer uncommon perspectives. Dull and boring gets old very quickly.

7. **Are they reliable?** Woody Allen said, "Showing up is 80 percent of life." Can your team players be counted on to be at work regularly? Are they responsible in taking care of their mental and physical health? Do they respect the health of others? Many construction jobs are dangerous and require the full attention of employees. What if someone was reckless and endangered themselves and others? I had just one rule when I was coaching basketball, and it was "Don't let your teammate down." This embodies reliability.

8. **Are they learners?** Every job requires ongoing learning. Do your team players seek out education and improvement, or is it like pulling teeth for you to get them to do any professional development? You want people who don't need to be told that learning is essential.

9. **Are they ambitious?** The word *ambitious*, unfortunately, is misconstrued as a negative. *Ambition* is defined as "an earnest desire for some type of achievement, and the willingness to strive for its attainment." You want people that have self-determination and an entrepreneurial spirit about their work.

10. **Do they trust?** Whenever I was picked on a playground team, I may not have been best buddies with the captain, yet I trusted him or her to lead the squad. Are your team players able to trust you and the other leaders to do the best for both the business and them? Although trust must often be earned over time, there

needs to be an initial level of faith to be successful.

Picking teams usually entails pursuing the positive traits of others. Sometimes, someone can fool you at interview time, or often, world and personal events may alter someone's motivation. Many other times, the fit is all wrong, and you must make tough decisions even with people you like. Focus first on what an ideal team and its players look like, as illustrated above. Then the harder part of leadership comes. . .

How to Extricate the Poison Within

A couple of years ago, I noticed a strange-looking sore right below Captain Jack's right eye. Captain Jack is not prone to complaining (unless a menacing rabbit has entered the property). The sore was bleeding slightly, eerily puffy, and a little scary for me. When Barb got home, we took a closer look at it (Barb is much more astute and empathetic about injuries because of her experience with our children's girlhood scrapes). On closer inspection, it looked like an abscess. We thought he might have been bitten by something. The following day, we made a hasty trip to the veterinarian.

Dr. Craig Adams at the Poulsbo Animal Clinic is Jack's physician, and he quickly diagnosed a different problem. Our feisty friend had broken his tooth. He had been chewing on a rocklike toy bone we had given him because all the other soft ones had been promptly destroyed. We wished we had chosen destroyed over broken! The tooth had developed an infection that went up through the cheek, punctured through the skin and fur, and eventually, manifested itself in the sore we saw.

Dr. Craig was quick to point out that this was a pretty tough dog. If it had been one of us humans, we'd have been delirious with pain and begging for immediate painkillers and surgery. Dr. Craig and I were amazed that not only was Jack not symptomatic outside of the visual sore, but he hadn't even lost his appetite or aptitude for eating. Dr. Craig gave us medications for the short term, and we scheduled surgery for the next week. As quickly as the ulcer had come, it went away; surgery was successful. Heck, Captain Jack didn't even need a cone of shame!

Infections are a poison. Once produced, the venom spreads to all parts of the infected area, and if left to its own devices, will compromise the entire body. Dogs (and humans) are susceptible to bodily infections and the poison they carry. We have doctors, medications, and treatments to help us get better. Business organizations and business professionals are also susceptible to venom that can be just as malignant if left untreated.

There are many things that can poison your team as individuals and collectively. They start small, but like an infection, can spread quickly, and left to their own devices, will consume your culture and damage your business.

The Invidious and Hidden Toxin

How do you know that you've been infected? Captain Jack had a hole boring through his face, so that was obvious. Similarly, your "infection" will be empirical. However, the problem is that often you're just not paying attention because it only hurts when it's visible, and then it might be too late.

Here are the painful warning signs for both your own career and the people you are responsible for.

You and Your Career:

- Apathy for your work
- Boredom
- Fear
- No passion
- Loss of "reward"
- Trepidation
- Anxiety
- Confusion
- Analysis paralysis
- Glass ceiling syndrome (you can't advance any higher)

Your Business:

- Constant drama and conflict between employees
- Lack of trust between management (you) and employees
- Rumors and innuendo
- High turnover rate
- Unsafe working environment
- Anemic communication between all areas of organization
- Bad leadership
- Inconsistent discipline and rules
- Apathy

So if these are the manifestations of the poison, what exactly is this infection causing them? There are three categories of poisons:

Figure 4.1

You: We always need to start by looking in the mirror first. Throughout this book, the theme of attitude will be ubiquitous. Attitude can sum up most of the cause for being unhappily stuck in your fenced in yard and unable to be Unleashed. Here's how you might poison your own water:

- **Negative thinking.** I define negative thinking as always expecting the worst, being cynical, and never accepting good fate as something other than luck. This negative thinking can manifest itself over years of boredom, unhappiness, lack of reward, or some other event. We rarely start out negative. Take a look at yourself. . .are you positive or negative?

- **Gloomy thinking.** While negative thinking is more contemptuous, gloomy thinking is more pessimistic. This is when the skies are always proverbially gray, when bad things "just happen to me," "I can't seem to ever get ahead. . . " While not normally malicious, you can become the party pooper on steroids!

- **Finger-pointing.** It's the mentality that it's always someone else's fault, the lack of personal responsibility necessary to own up to one's situation. I saw this attitude many times in both my career as a basketball coach and my stint as a school board member. Parents would often blame others for their children's "problems." It was always the teacher, principal, coach, other team, other students, etc. Instead of being answerable to themselves, they found someone else to pin the blame on. You see that in your organization and in your personal life. You don't want to see it in yourself!

- **Complacency.** This one is tough to diagnose, especially when it's you. I define complacency as "content to the point of going through the motions and not caring about the consequences." Complacency is a symptom of being caught in a *success trap*.

The "success trap" occurs when you are rewarded and lauded for something that you're good at but actually dislike. This is how jobs get in the way of careers, and necessary evils come to impede our lives. Let your internal gyroscope tell you what's right for you, not external influences.

~ Alan Weiss

It's so easy to get caught up into the daily routine that you simply lose interest and your passion sinks like heavy boots in a muddy field. It never gets so deep that you can't move, but the effort gets harder and harder over time. Finding this rooted in you is difficult, if not almost impossible. Listen to the people around you because they will in some form or fashion let you know.

- **Arrogance.** There is a big difference between confidence and arrogance. Too many people I talk to believe they are one and the same, and they are not. While there might appear to be a thin line between the two of them, it takes a pretty good leap to cross. *Arrogance* revolves around smugness. It's the belief that you already know the answers and you don't need to learn anymore. *Confidence* is the knowledge that you are really good at what you do (maybe even elite) and that you're a worthy person. You also know that you can always learn more from just about anyone and you seek to constantly improve and enhance yourself and your career.

  Be full of confidence. Be wary of arrogance. The former will allow you to be free to more fully advance your career and enrich your life. The latter will poison your thinking and your life.

Others: In the examples above, I discussed taking responsibility for your own situation, your actions, and your thinking. While this is true, you may be responsible for others who cause chaos and are out of your control. When this happens, YOU then must again gain control and be responsible for whom you choose to associate with. Being able to accomplish this is one of the key traits of Unleashed leadership.

All five of the bullet points mentioned above not only apply to your personal assessment, *they apply to assessing the people that you are responsible for.* Go back and review the points, and replace *you* with *them*.

While you might correctly argue that there are employees and others in your life whom you simply can't eliminate, I contend you have more power and control than you think. The first step is always to influence. The second step requires training and coaching. Sometimes, the employees themselves may just "self-select" their way out of the company, and you may have to help them reach that end quickly. Collaborative leadership wants to pull the best out of people but acknowledges that it won't always happen and that then steps need to be taken. It requires strong confidence and courage to evict the *fun suckers* before they create a dangerous poison in your company.

Extra Point: Fun suckers are people who suck all the fun out of your world at any given moment. They are like a dark cloud that engulfs a beautiful blue sky. I recall watching the most ugly, dark, and menacing black cloud while playing golf in central Washington. It was a splendid summer day, and while standing on the ninth tee, I saw, off in the distance, this ominous cloud moving towards us with great alacrity. Within fifteen minutes, it was over us, and the golf course management summoned all the golfers inside. This one cloud basically sucked the golfers off of the course and into hiding. Fun suckers will suck out your energy, your passion, and your fun. And remember, "work" is best performed when it's fun!

Let's not take ourselves so seriously. Life is meant to be fun, even in our work and career. If it's not fun, you have a problem because one of the factors listed in the "You" section earlier will quickly haunt you. So make sure you identify those incurable fun suckers and assure that they are either dismissed or mitigated.

Fun suckers live in all facets of your life. For the sake of brevity, we will focus on the business side of the equation. However, don't allow family and friends to spread that venom. You don't have a personal and a professional life. You have a life. And that one life is affected by everything.

Here are my five simple rules to extricate the invidious poison to your company:

1. **Take a hard look at yourself and make sure that you're not the problem.** This takes courage, self-confidence, and scrutiny. It's basically a soul-searching experience. Often, you'll need help from a coach, mentor, or colleague. However, it's where you need to start to determine if your leadership, behavior, and modeling is enhancing or hurting your business. The very best business leaders and professionals are humble and vulnerable enough to self-assess without reserve. In and of itself, that quality is essential in being Unleashed.

2. **Deal with conflict immediately.** I've known very nice, very smart, and savvy business owners who avoided conflict like my daughters avoid snakes, spiders, and ugly shoes. Conflict among employees especially must be dealt with swiftly, and with skill. If you're not adept in this area, find someone in your organization who is. Conflict left unabated is the quickest form of infection. Refusing to deal with conflict says more about one's level of self-confidence than just about any other factor. Many people avoid conflict because they are scared of not being liked. Remove that obstacle and you should, at least, have an easier time confronting conflict. Remember that, as a leader, you're not there to be an employee's friend. You're there to make them the best they possibly can be. As with raising children, that balancing act of love and discipline can lead to conflict. The greater good is always the other person's improvement.

3. **Take the pulse.** The "pulse" is the heartbeat of your operation. Are your employees happy? Are they engaged in the business, or simply punching the clock? Are you providing a challenging and rewarding experience, or are they bored and seeking new employment while you aren't looking? You need to be skilled at observation and asking questions—demanding honest answers and respecting them—and able to deal rapidly with areas that need fixing.

4. **Have fun.** I was once a guest at an office that had a foosball table in the middle of all the cubicles. There were other stations in and around the work area meant to offer a respite from labor. The break area offered unique coffees, teas, and other snacks. No wonder this company is consistently ranked as one of the top places to work in the Seattle-area. What do you do to promote a fun environment? Gone are the days of working people until they drop. You need to balance a mix of fun with the hard work that is being done. You will find that, by doing so, the efforts during work, as well as the results, are better.

5. **Stay vigilant.** You can't do this self-analysis and clean up just once and forget about it. The poison has a slippery way of trying to work itself back in. You must be vigilant. That requires scheduling some of these behaviors and activities into your calendar and then following through. That means making real changes that become part of your culture and are sustainable. To repeat Peter Drucker's wisdom from the previous chapter, "Culture eats strategy for breakfast." Make sure you're eating a healthy breakfast! I didn't wait to take Captain Jack into see Dr. Craig, as I was scared that doing so would be deleterious to his health. His open wound was as clear to me as your issues should be to you, yet too often, yours are ignored or swept under the rug. Stop sweeping and start acting. By investing your time and effort into my five simple rules, you will join Jack on the road to good health and eating crunchy dog treats.

Helping Others Dispose of the Poison

If you're in a position of leadership as the business owner, executive, manager, or even as a coach/mentor for someone, then you have a duty and obligation to help others be the best they can be. The information you just read will be of help to others, and aside from giving others this book to read, you can offer your own sage advice based on personal experiences that are unique to only you.

Here are my **7 *Tactical Strategies*** to helping you assist those in your employ, your direct reports, and hopefully, even those in your circle of family and friends, to dispose of their own poison within:

1. **Become a storyteller.** People learn best when they are engaged and listening intently. The best way to achieve both is to tell stories. We all love hearing a good story because it helps us recall our own experiences. Once that is accomplished, it's much easier for us to have those very important "ah-ha!" moments. As the storyteller, that's your goal. You don't have to be a professional speaker to do this. If you can tell stories to your children, you can tell them to adults. Get some help, join a local Toastmasters club for practice, and then begin to add some *sizzle* to that steak!

2. **Use your own life experiences**. You've had the opportunity to read my own personal stories throughout this book. In this chapter alone, I've shared experiences as metaphor and allegory to make you think more deeply and understand the points of emphasis. What significant experiences have impacted your life that you can use? What seemingly small events are capable of packing a big punch when telling your story? That old adage of "tell a story, make a point" is as true today as ever. It's an easy concept to follow and repeat.

3. **Be vulnerable.** This is a tough one for many of you. The difference it makes to those listening to you is remarkable. We've all made mistakes in life that we've learned from. I have my own long "laundry list" to draw from! The importance of being vulnerable is two-fold. First, it shows you're human and can admit it. People respect that from their leaders. It allows for the very real emotions of compassion and trust. Second, it shows that you don't think you are "special." People crave learning how to overcome adversity. They want to learn from you and how you did it. If you never share your own foibles, how can they possibly improve?

4. **Use self-deprecating humor.** Humor is essential when telling

stories and making points. If you don't believe me, watch a few hours of television and count the number of humorous ads as compared to the non-humorous ones. People learn when they laugh. Humor can be tricky depending on your audience. One thing is certain, however. If you make fun of yourself, nobody will be offended! Aside from really charming your audience ("audience" is loose here—might be one person), you will also demonstrate that you don't take yourself too seriously. This is a characteristic that comes in handy regularly in leadership.

5. **Be candid.** *Tough love* is necessary to help others. I know that there have been many times in my life that I've avoided specificity in advising family and friends because I was worried about hurting their feelings. It's much easier for me to be tough with clients (not that I want to hurt their feelings) because they hired me to be straight with them so they can succeed more quickly. *Tough love* isn't about being mean or insensitive. It's truly about having the best interest of the other person at heart and wanting to help them. Often, people need a bit of a "shake-up" to catch their attention. The only way change occurs is when you capture that attention, and tough, honest advice does that.

I will never forget one particular meeting with Alan Weiss and my mastermind group in San Francisco. At the end of the day, we asked Alan to tell each of us specific ways that we could improve. Alan knew all of us well, so this was pretty easy for him. When he got to me, he said, "Dan, you're *terminally* nice." This wasn't a compliment. He went on to explain that I needed to become more assertive and find ways to be more contrarian to get people's attention. I wasn't there to be "liked"; I was there to be influential. I needed to shake things up and that meant becoming more forceful. He could have danced around the topic in an effort to be nicer himself, but neither of us had time for that. I appreciated his candor, and it made an immediate impact on me.

6. **Be empathetic.** There is a difference between the words *sym-pathetic* and *empathetic. Sympathetic* is about feeling sorry for someone else's misfortune. *Empathetic* is about truly *understanding and feeling* the plight and situation of someone else. There is an affinity, a comprehension that you understand and can relate. This is so important when mentoring others. As a leader, you are automatically a mentor, so this is vital. Having the ability to let the other person know that you truly *understand* and *feel* their issue is necessary in building trust and rapport. You may have experienced a similar situation in your life or career, so you can attest to the difficulty or pain. Empathy is needed to help others know you genuinely care about them.

   Important: Being empathetic and showing *tough love* are NOT mutually exclusive. In fact, when used in tandem, they are compelling. Just because you feel empathy for another doesn't preclude you from being brutally honest. Use that empathy in your tone and language, yet be specific, pithy, and to the point. Leaders who can master this talent are very special.

7. **Provide sustainability.** Each of us has undoubtedly at some point sought help from others, received it, and used it. Then, after a few weeks or months, we drifted back into our old habits. *Gravitational pull* at work! The best leaders know they need to monitor that advice they gave by providing a framework for sustainability. Set metrics with your protégé, create timelines and "check backs," and determine ways to be accessible to assure improvement and long-term growth.

Anger Management

This entire chapter has been dedicated to the successful expulsion of poisonous thinking, behaviors, and activities that stymie us from being truly Unleashed. There is a common thread that runs through most of the "poisons." That is anger.

I'm not talking about the anger you feel when you stub your toe or bang your thumb with a hammer. Nor am I talking about the anger you face when your favorite sports team loses (I've been known to fly into fits of anger with the Seahawks, Mariners, Sonics, and Huskies). I am talking about anger that is rooted in relationships—both professional and personal.

My wife Barb is not only beautiful and talented, but she's also pretty smart. As far back as I can remember in our adult life, she has preached to our daughters (and too many times to me!) that anger stems from your own anger at yourself, not the other person or situation.

Right after the penultimate season of my high school basketball coaching career, I received a hand-delivered letter from one of the parents in my basketball community. This person was someone I had known well, and I had coached his daughter in youth leagues. When he arrived at my place of business to deliver this letter, he was quite somber and said, "You might want to read this alone." The crux of this four-page letter was that a group of parents with kids coming up into high school were not happy that the program wasn't winning more games, and that I was the proximate cause of this travesty. The letter forcefully implied that if I didn't immediately resign, there would be some tremendous storm of community pressure that would come thundering down on me. What was most hurtful was that I knew this person and considered him a friend. In fact, the other signers (none of whom had had kids play for me in high school) were also people I knew and thought were friends.

The drama didn't last long. I wanted to continue coaching, my family and employer fully backed me, and the community pressure turned out to be a very small number of agitators. I coached one more season (one of our best) and left due to the founding of my own consulting practice, which required my full attention. In fact, all those athletes who, according to the letter, "would never play" for me? All did.

The story should have ended there.

But I stayed angry with the particular parent who was the ringleader and had written and delivered the scathing letter. I stopped frequenting his business out of spite. The thought of him made me angry and acrimonious. And I defiantly intended to not let that go.

The problem was this: I was allowing that person to rent space in my brain. That space in my brain was definitely needed for other more important matters! To make matters even more interesting, I doubt this guy even knew I was harboring this anger. While a year later, even though I didn't have him or his family as part of my life, the anger still hounded me.

I'm not sure what the tipping point was for me. Maybe it was something Barb said, so let's just give her the credit. The remaining anger I felt really wasn't aimed at him. While I felt hurt and betrayed, that part passed pretty quickly. The anger emanated from me. I was angry with myself for not winning more games and avoiding this embarrassment. I was angry with myself for allowing myself to be hurt because I was trying so hard to be "liked." That was the anger that remained and was still being foisted upon this guy.

I made the decision to stop being angry. This is much more intentional than forgiving and forgetting. I would never forget, but that's because I'm still young enough to have a decent memory! I had to commit to no longer letting it make me angry. I had actually forgiven him in my own mind, but had yet to release that forgiveness to myself. The actual steps I took were to reenter his business and simply "shop." While I didn't purchase anything, I didn't need to. The mere act of going in was liberating. The intentionality of allowing myself to stop being angry with myself basically booted him out of the rental unit in my brain!

Look back on the times you've been unhappy in your life. Was anger a part of that? Was the anger aimed at others, or maybe truly at you? Are you still angry with someone else and is it causing rancor now?

This is a *tough love* segment of this chapter. I understand the effects of anger and so do you. There is often something deeper involved when dealing with anger. It takes hard work, humility, and decisiveness to remove. I suggest that if there are people and situations in your life where "poison" remains, that you take a hard look to see if anger is a partner in it. My guess is that it may be the catalyst to the unhappiness. The sooner you can dispose of that anger, the sooner you will have more space available in your brain to become Unleashed!

Building Your Program From Within
Creating a Repeatable Message

One of the things that most impresses me about the Seattle Seahawks under the current Pete Carroll regime is their "messaging." It seems that every player interviewed will espouse the company line by parroting the same themes. You hear comments like "Every game is a championship opportunity," or "The separation is in the preparation" ad nauseam. The difference with the Seahawks players is that they truly believe what they are saying. They aren't just preaching the company line; they are genuinely living it.

One of the insurance agencies I once worked for decided to create a mission statement. This mission statement took an inordinate amount of time to develop to assure that every single word was considered for impact. One of the principal owners decided that he wanted all the employees to memorize the mission statement and would incentivize us with a one hundred dollar cash reward. One by one, over the following weeks, employees would enter the conference room and robotically regurgitate the mission statement to earn their one hundred dollars.

I refused. It wasn't that I didn't want to be a team player. I believed the value of the agency. I just didn't think I needed to mindlessly memorize a statement that I would forget within the next two days. That would be the same thing that happened to me in eighth grade chemistry. That principal owner was under the mistaken notion that uttering words repeatedly would produce some sort of magical muscle memory. All it did was get him to spend money better invested elsewhere. The reason: he was forcing it down our throats rather than creating an environment and organizational culture that encouraged the mission and vision. When this happens, you either fit in or you don't, and it is obvious to everyone.

How do you go about creating this culture where the company line becomes more than just a recitation of fancy words? Let's be clear, I am NOT talking mission statements. I'm encouraging you to consider this your vision and your company culture. It's more of a feeling than words strung together. With that, allow me to give you some words to work by. . .

Let's go back to the playground rules, and I will give you my *7 Rules for Championship Messaging*:

1. **Be real.** Sounds crazy, but it's the most important. If you don't believe in your message, nobody else will. If it's someone else's words, then it's not real. The messaging that comes out of your mouth must come from your heart and you must believe it.

2. **Be pithy.** Short and sweet. If it's too complicated, it will be forgotten.

3. **Be consistent.** This applies to your words and your actions.

4. **Engage your leaders.** They need to be saying the same things. They can't be robots just mimicking you. They have to also believe in the culture.

5. **Prove it.** When we played H-O-R-S-E on my basketball hoop at home, when you got to the point where you beat the other person, you actually had to "prove" it to seal the game. That meant you had to make the basket again or force the other person to miss again. In this case, you must "prove" your message over and over until it becomes ingrained and trusted.

6. **Be patient.** Change takes time. So does building a culture. For Pete Carroll and the Seahawks, it was almost three years into his regime before it started really bearing fruit. It shouldn't take that long for you, but as they say, "Rome wasn't built in a day!"

7. **Have fun.** Another ubiquitous theme in this book. Life is too short and you spend too much time with your colleagues to be miserable. If you're having fun at work, your employees and team are likely to as well.

This sounds easy, but it's not. As humans, we have our good and bad days, and consistency is an awful tough thing to. . .well. . .be consistent with! Just don't give up. There will be failings for both you and your team. Learn from them and adjust. Ignoring missteps, allowing unwanted behavior, and a lack of discipline in this area are lethal to building your program. In the final analysis, as a leader, you will be observed closely and judged. People will try to see if you are what you say you are. It's the hardest part of being a leader; ask any politician or Fortune 500 CEO!

Commit to making changes to your messaging and vision, and then get started. You don't have to wait to be "perfect" because that won't ever happen. You will find yourself waiting forever. Follow the seven rules and get started. Ask your key people to join you and share in the company vision. This is a terrific way to get them intricately engaged. You will be glad you did.

A Captain Jack Extra Point
Joie de Vivre

I like kids. As far as I can tell, humans are at their best when they are only about four and a half feet off the ground. The taller they get, the more complex and less intelligent they become. I guess it may have something to do with verticality. Dogs and kids are both close the ground.

When I go for a walk, kids come running to greet me. There is never a lack of assertiveness. They run first, then they ask Dan if they can say hello and pet me. The fascinating thing is that they ask the question in such a way that they expect the answer to be yes. It's as if they will it. It's the same way with dogs. When Bella and I bark that it's time to eat dinner, we literally will Dan to get off his butt and feed us. It's a skill.

Kids have this joie de vivre about them (yes, I know a little French. . .at least the words that are important for me as a scribe). They seldom seem to be curtailed by minutiae that stand in the way of their objectives. Even a mother calling from the distance doesn't make an immediate impact. The objective of fun is always at the root of their behavior.

Fun is a funny word. Adults tend to think of this as only available during discretionary time. Fun can and should be had in all you do. That includes your work, your play, your learning, your relationships, and your hobbies. I have fun when I chase a ball or vigorously rub my back up against the heat vent. The routes are different, but the objective is the same.

My words of wisdom for you, my human friends, they are this: At one time you were children, so I know this joie de vivre still lives in you somewhere. Find it. Use it for good and don't hide it. You never know when that ball you are chasing will roll outside your comfort zone and you will need to have the courage and the passion to finish the route. It's not that complicated. If kids and dogs can do it, there is hope for you.

Just saying. . .
Captain Jack

Calling the Plays

TURNING PLAYERS INTO PLAYMAKERS

Dogs are hunters by nature. Captain Jack is certainly no exception. Jack Russell terriers were bred to seek and capture (and subsequently exterminate) rodents, snakes, and other varmints. Captain Jack is an expert snake stalker.

A few years ago, Barb and I were in New York City. I had a business trip, and we decided to make an event out of it since Barb had never been to the Big Apple. We had been out for the day and came back to the hotel to prepare to go to our first Broadway show. That's when the text came in.

We have a very competent and professional dog sitter. Sue comes to the house and not only cares for Captain Jack and Bella, she also doubles as a house sitter. We've availed ourselves of her services for years. She is a dog authority par excellence. So when I received her text, it drew a substantial amount of curiosity. . .

"Jack has traumatized me for life!"

That was it. Without waiting to see if more was coming, I immediately called her. I knew Jack was safe, but he had obviously done something that might end up costing me thousands of dollars in therapy bills for Sue.

As it turns out, Sue had taken Captain Jack out into the front yard for his midday "elimination." Upon inspection of the yard, Captain had discovered a snake hidden in the juniper bush. With astonishing agility, he lunged into the juniper and came out triumphantly with the snake clenched in his mouth. For as mighty a deed as this might be for canines, Sue was unimpressed and horrified. In fact, she freaked out. She immediately began tugging on the leash in an effort to force Jack to drop the snake. Jack had a vice-like grip. In her words, "He shook the snake to death right in front of my eyes!" After a brief struggle akin to an angler trying to reel in the big one, Jack lost his grip, and the snake plopped to the ground. Sue darted inside, pulling a clearly unhappy dog in behind her. She said, "I left the snake for you."

That she did. When we returned home four days later, it was still in the yard (obviously, the dogs were taken elsewhere for their daily constitutionals). It had a kink in it that resembled a garden hose that had gotten caught on a rock.

As I said, dogs are hunters. When Captain Jack spots something he is bred to hunt, he wastes no time or thought in going after it. It's called a "predator mentality." Somewhere along evolution's trail, we humans lost that predator mentality. Now, too many of us recoil at opportunity for fear of rejection or failure, from lack of self-confidence, or because we have no idea on how to start. We have a tendency to linger around familiar settings because they feel safe and secure—and we forget that we've been Unleashed. Before long, we actually trap ourselves in our own self-imposed yard and never maximize our own talents.

You may recognize this trap within yourself. As a leader, you self-assess first and then help your team. You remain calm. It's similar to the flight attendant on an airplane instructing you to put your own mask on first in the event of loss of air pressure in the cabin. You can't help others if you're not breathing yourself. The rest of this chapter will focus on the latter. How do you help your employees overcome the fears they may harbor and pull out that *predator mentality* within each of them?

Breaking It Down
Defining Roles & Responsibilities

Executive coaching and mentoring has been a popular buzz phrase in the business world for the past several years. From the military to the boardroom, mandatory tutoring and guidance has been issued as an edict. In fact, I've been called on in many instances to "train the trainers." There are hazards in trying to implement coaching and mentoring programs for those that are doing it just because they are required to, or because they think they should. Let's examine five specific problems.

Problem #1—There is no clear definition of the difference between mentoring and coaching. My definition is clear—mentoring is a reaction to a request for help; coaching is a guided process to rapidly reach a level of competence or skill. There will be more details on each of these concepts later in this chapter.

Problem # 2—Roles, responsibilities, and expectations are also not clearly defined and explained. More on this shortly.

Problem #3—Training the trainer is often not considered. I've been fortunate to work with sophisticated executives that understood that skill development, practice, and confidence in the process were required prior to jumping into a formal program. Using an outside resource who is experienced in training others in this area is highly recommended.

Problem #4—Limited resources. The availability of actual coaches and mentors that have the time to help others and still do their own work is a challenge. This is especially true in many small businesses. We will address this soon.

Problem #5—Buy-in. This is buy-in from everyone—upper leadership, managers and supervisors, and employees. This isn't simple. There must be a commitment to the process, a willingness to be nimble, the dexterity to make adjustments as needed, and a belief that these engagements will lead to an enhanced work environment, better productivity, and reduced churn.

Defining roles and responsibilities is usually the initial step in the process. In and of itself, it has its own three-step path:

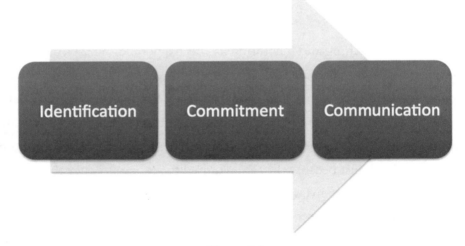

Figure 5.1

Identification: Identification of *who* should be mentors and coaches comes first. Let's spend a little time with a deeper examination.

Mentors and coaches might (and most probably will) be completely different individuals. This identification requires a candid assessment and search.

Mentors should NOT have direct control or managerial functions over their mentee. Mentors should be peer-level colleagues who have experience, expertise, and knowledge that would benefit someone with similar career aspirations. If you have a sales team and are adding a new employee in this division, you should identify a skilled sales professional to be a mentor, rather than the sales manager. As you will learn in the next section, mentors are stable and discerning "ears and voices" that bear no anxiety to the mentees concerning their job statuses.

Coaches tend to be more active guides in a process related to building specific skills. This is often a supervisory or managerial position. More on this later.

Identification must be the first step because you need to assess who your team of teachers actually is. If you skip this part, you risk poor placements, bad relationships, and a program that will soon slide into obscurity. If you make this a priority and do well, you're setting up a rewarding situation for everyone involved, including positive results for your organization.

Commitment: As previously mentioned, commitment is critical. The fastest way to hijack a new program is to force people unwilling to be part of the process into action. It is clearly evident when someone is coerced into being a coach or mentor.

How do you gain commitment? As a leader, you must exert influence, not force. We humans most often care about what's in it for us. This isn't a pessimistic comment, rather a reality that we all want to gain some reward for our investment. Using messaging that creates positive outcomes is necessary. What are the positive outcomes in your business or organization? They might include:

- Increased financial compensation
- Personal growth and development (every coach will tell you that they gain more from coaching engagements than their protégées).
- Sense of pride. Being asked to mentor or coach may be a high honor for someone in your company. Never underestimate the power of praise.
- Reduction in work. In my experience, most pushback is around time commitments. If these are addressed and the potential coach or mentor doesn't feel anxious about an increased workload, they are more likely to commit.
- Recognition. Maybe you have a company newsletter, awards, or different honors. Recognition is a big motivator to many people.
- Potential advancement. With increased responsibility and skills might come opportunities to qualify for new positions.

In the end, you may find one, or you might identify many factors. In order to get people to commit and dedicate themselves to a program, there must be some reward in it for them. You need to (in advance) put a plan into place to be able to give these folks confidence, security, and reward.

Communication: I've seen well-intentioned plans fail miserably when communications weren't strong. This communication strategy takes planning and effort to deliver your message in a multitude of ways. Everyone hears news a little differently. You've all played that game where you sit in a circle and one morsel of information gets started around by whispering it to the next person. By the time it's reached the end, it has little semblance to the original message. Imagine how this plays out along water coolers and cubicles!

Create a document that illustrates why and how your internal program will work. Detail specifically those roles and responsibilities, make sure everyone knows who is participating, explain time lines and expectations, and provide a place for employees to go and ask questions, get advice, or just vent frustration. Hold a forum where people can ask questions both individually and as a group. Affording an opportunity for collective questions and wisdom often leads to bonding, and many times, to great ideas.

Communications is a fluid concept. Once implemented, it is bound to change, even if it was perfect in the beginning. Be prepared, as a leader in your company, to make adjustments to any communications plan and then (you guessed it), communicate it to everyone verbally (in both written and spoken forms).

When Coaching Your Team Makes Sense

You read my definition of coaching previously in this chapter. To remind you, I defined coaching as "a guided process to rapidly reach a level of competence or skill."

In 2007, I was competing in the Toastmasters International speech contest. There were over 22,000 contestants around the planet vying for the title of World Champion of Public Speaking. I had what I considered a pretty good speech, and one that could get me to a lofty level. I wrote it myself based on the story of teaching my daughter Mindy how to drive a car. The speech was titled "STOP" and gave a detailed account of a near accident in a high school parking lot.

As a former high school basketball coach, I understood the value of coaching, so I hired the 2001 World Champion of Public Speaking, Darren LaCroix to coach me for the contest. The timing was such that we only had minimal discussion prior to my first leg in the process, the club contest. Fortunately, I won that contest handily. . .I was the ONLY contestant. All I had to do was not exceed the time and disqualify myself!

Immediately pursuant to that speech, I attended a workshop in Dallas that Darren was giving along with two other former world champions, Ed Tate and Craig Valentine. We decided to hold a more significant meeting in person while we were there together. I was pretty upbeat. My staggering victory gave me a burgeoning confidence that "STOP" was my manifest destiny! I figured Darren would love it, pat me on the head for my triumph the previous week, and give me a few pointers for the road.

That didn't happen. Darren quickly pointed out that each step in the process would be more difficult (especially with the inclusion of competitors). And what was worse, he didn't like my open. He pondered deeply over what he didn't like about it. The answer finally came to him, and it suddenly burst from his mouth. He recommended that I begin on stage silently, appearing to agonize and fret over something. Then, with great intensity and amplification, exclaim "STOP!" and throw out my arms as if to ward off an impending collision. He felt that this was the best way to draw in the audience through increasing curiosity and building to a climax that uttered merely one word. They would have to know the rest of the story.

I loved it and said I would implement it after the next round of the area contest. I didn't feel like I had time to rehearse all the changes. His response startled me. He looked at me with an icy intensity and firmly proclaimed, "NO!" He went on to say, "The area contest will be harder, and you need your best. I believe with all my heart that THIS open will be necessary. You have to learn it and use it. I don't care when the contest is. . ."

I decided to listen to my coach. I made the change, and it was as brilliant as he surmised. The speech ended up being my most popular and successful ever. I won the district competition, which advanced me to the international semifinal in Rancho Cordova, California. Unfortunately, I couldn't use that speech at further contests, and my bid for the finals ended there. Regardless, the speech was a success, not only as a competition speech but also to the audience. I will never forget one of the other contestants at the district level approaching me after the announcement of winners (she finished in second place). She said, "I just loved your speech. It moved me so much that I am going to give my father a call when I get home. He taught me how to drive, and I never thanked him for that. I am now." That may have been the best reward I received in the entire process. Without Darren's coaching, I may have never advanced past that area round and competed further or influenced others.

Darren's role was to lay the foundation for a specific purpose. In this case, it was creating and delivering an award-winning speech. He guided the process, gave me homework, demanded accountability, and was accessible throughout the process.

That's coaching. In your business, this might mean the coaching of whatever methodology you offer. That means:

- Skills coaching as it relates to building your product
- Behavior modification
- Professional growth, like writing, speaking, or selling

This very often is the role of a direct supervisor or manager who has mastered this skill or behavior and will directly guide one through that process. Coaching most generally has a life span. In mentoring, you will read that this relationship can go on forever. In coaching, that would mean that the skill or behavior never took. That means one of two things—the coaching was bad or the person wasn't suited to the job. Regardless, at some point, coaching needs to end, and ongoing support (mentoring), begin. That takes us to the next section. . .

When Mentoring Others Makes Sense

I love to walk a golf course. It's how I grew up in the game and how

I most fondly recall why I came to love it. As courses have become more complicated based on housing developments and increased length between greens and tees, riding a cart has become more necessary. In over three decades of playing the game, I'd never used a caddy (although I had been one on many occasions) until August of 2011.

I was in Bogotá, Colombia at a major executive conference where I was one of the keynote speakers. It was the first trip back to my mom's native land in exactly forty years. It became an ideal opportunity to mix business with the pleasure of reacquainting myself with my family after four decades. One of my cousins is married to a newspaper executive and fellow insatiable golfer. He invited me to join him and another cousin on the links at his country club. How could I refuse?

To my surprise and delight, Jorge's country club allowed no golf carts. Instead they provided caddies. According to Jorge, this was not unique. He said that even in municipal courses, you never saw carts. He hooked me up with an extraordinary young man named Sebastian as my caddy.

One of the problems of playing less golf as I got older was that my ability to quickly fix swing ailments had diminished drastically. The results were predictable. Basically, I would keep doing what I was doing and keep getting the same results. One of the advantages of having a savvy caddy is that he or she is expert in assessing swing failures. Sebastian was no exception. He quickly deduced early in the round that my inconsistent shots were a result of not "finishing" my swing. A proper "finish" means that the golfer has accelerated through the ball and has correctly shifted his or her weight to ensure the accurate flight of the ball. The consequences of not finishing are that the club head strikes the ball with an "open face" and it shoots out as a *slice*. This is termed "blocking." This is bad.

Sebastian informed me of the issue, yet didn't leave it to chance that I would execute the solution. He would start by making sure I was lined up correctly and say, "Okay." Then he would walk away directly behind me with a strong command of "FINISH!" That word was the last thing I heard before each swing. It was the catalyst for me to stay focused on one thing. . .the finish.

I am certain Sebastian's guidance and attention to every detail saved me six strokes that day. Heck, he even found two balls in play that I had given up for lost. If I had the power to stuff him in my suitcase and bring him home, I would have done it. There's no doubt my handicap would have plummeted into single digits! It made a huge difference in my play, my score, and my enjoyment of the round that day.

Sebastian was my mentor. A coach is one who works on your exact swing in practice settings, assigns homework to improve your new skills, and assiduously creates a game plan for long-term success. A mentor is a reminder and a "just in time" guide.

The reason I say that Sebastian was my mentor was because he was there in the thick of the battle. He would offer tidbits of quick fix advice and provide me with positive thoughts and reminders. He wasn't a coach. . .he was basically helping me to do what I had already learned and knew about my game.

In the business world, mentoring is critical. In the previous section, we discussed how coaching builds the foundation. It is very specific and usually has a set life span. Mentoring can be forever. It's the natural progression out of a fruitful coaching experience.

Mentoring makes sense in your business when:

1. **Coaching is finished.** What is needed is a resource to continue to ask questions of, get advice from, role-play situations with, or just vent to. In a consulting situation, it's common to have the coach and mentor be the same person. In a management scenario, it might not be. A lot depends on the size of the organization.

2. **Confidence is gained.** Once confidence is in place, mentoring can be even more effective. I've had many situations where mentor clients lacked the confidence to even call and ask questions. That defeats the purpose! Confidence allows for more vulnera-

bility and growth.

3. **Accountability is desired.** Often in a work environment, accountability is needed. A mentor can be that accountability partner that is necessary to monitor and ensure progress.

4. **Skills are honed.** In the business world, it is frequently the case that coaching on skills is a necessary first step. Once these skills have been built, a mentor can be that "go to" person that has the quick answer to a short question or need for clarity.

5. **Peace of mind is needed.** This is for the mentee's sake. I have clients who are confident, skilled, and accountable. That being said, they still want that peace of mind that they can go to someone they trust to quickly gain advice. This is in no way a crutch. It should be viewed more as "assurance insurance."

Mentoring can be a valuable component of any business. I normally recommend that supervisors and managers don't mentor those who directly report to them. If the mentees are having challenges with the supervisor, where can they go for advice? Rather, mentors should have knowledge about the business or job in question that can easily be transferred to another person outside their direct purview.

Rubber Meeting Road
All About That Action. . .

This section is the one that will try and pull this all together for you. I hope that I've done an adequate job defining the difference between coaching and mentoring. To be sure, let's put it into action. . .

Whenever you hire someone new, it's with the fervent hope that it works out well. Nobody goes into a new hire and hopes for the worst. The cost to bring in new people, train them, wait for their growth, and then finally reap rewards is hefty. Experts estimate that it's eighteen months. You do the math with your hires. You are seeking not only a significant ROI (Return on Investment), but also a sizeable ROT (Return on Time). That ROT is like the homely cousin to ROI; it never gets discussed yet is still an important part of the family. Time is valuable, and unlike money, you can't make more of it.

This is how a successfully implemented "onboarding" program for any new employee that includes a formal coaching/mentoring plan might look:

- Hiring process that includes several levels of interviews with multiple internal interviewers. It might begin with an initial phone call to weed out those who are obviously not fits. The next stages can move to different interviews, each due to the success of the previous one.

- Check referrals and prior employers. Don't ignore this because you think nobody will be candid. They usually are, and you never know what you will learn.

- Do some level of testing. Especially if your hire has specific skills they must demonstrate, you need to see what kind of "game" they are brining to your "court."

- Once through the hiring process, you need to head to the human resources part. Make sure the new hires get all their HR work done immediately. Your HR manager will love you for it, and it eliminates a lot of headaches later.

- You can run the coaching and mentoring processes concurrently. Coaching is about *skill building*. Mentoring is about *help*. Coaching is *short-term*; mentoring can be *long-term*.

- Have a mentor and a coach assigned. If you have budget and resources for only one, opt for mentoring. Note: Depending on your industry that might change. You will know best.

- Make sure all introductions and expectations are communicated by you to add validity.

- Stay in the loop. Ask both mentor and mentee for updates and reports on how things are progressing.

Expectations should center on several factors. These can be part of any initial strategy session around implementing a program. The following are my recommendations and basic metrics. Feel free to make this right for your specific business:

- **Access.** I suggest unlimited access during the business day.
- **Response Time.** There should be an agreement that the mentee should not expect the mentor to respond immediately. Voice- and email are acceptable (outside of a crisis, and you may need to define this too). Phone and text request responses can be within ninety minutes, and email, within four hours.
- **Actual Responses.** For a mentor, these are responses to specific questions. I recommend those I train to simply answer the question asked. Too often, we elaborate beyond need and waste everyone's time. Tell them what they need to know, not everything you know! For coaches, responses should be similar since it's outside of a regular coaching session.
- **Duration.** I think mentoring should be at least six months. Coaching duration will depend on what is being coached, and you will be the best to judge that. A good rule of thumb is at least three months.
- **Issues.** Be prepared by talking about potential problems. Discuss preferred ways to communicate, sensitive areas, personal idiosyncrasies, and anything else that could negatively affect the relationship. You can usually detect a bad match within the first thirty days.
- **Boss Time.** As a leader (assuming you're not the coach or mentor), you need to keep apprised of your employees' progress. As mentioned earlier, you don't need to know everything they are discussing. A straightforward "How are things going?" will suffice.
- **Coaching.** There will need to be additional conversation around what the coaching entails as it relates to "homework," regular sessions, the frequency of sessions, and discussion items.

I highly recommend you find some training for your coaches and mentors. There are a number of qualified consultants out there who can help you. Find one and get him or her to train your people in the following areas:

1. **Listening skills.** This is most important and, often, the most egregiously ignored. Listening and being in the moment is a learned skill. For some it comes easier than for others.

2. **Questioning skills.** The best coaches and mentors ask questions more than they give "advice." As a parent, I know I was very good at giving advice and declarations. I could have been much more effective had I used powerful questioning tools. Watch any television drama that includes interrogation scenes. Listen to the questions. While they aren't "real," they are based off the same practices.

3. **Empathy.** My daughters once dubbed me "Mr. Insensitive." Okay, that's par for the course with fathers, I think. As a mentor or coach, empathy is necessary. It's important for mentors and coaches to be viewed as caring about situations and people. Believe it or not, you can practice empathy.

4. **Practice.** There is no better way to be prepared for any conversation that might arise than to practice with your peers. Role-playing should be part of any monthly group meetings to continue to advance skills.

5. **Balance.** There will always be challenges with balancing work and mentoring/coaching. Even the very best relationships will have this, so it's best to be prepared. Being trained in how to deal with these demands in advance makes a huge difference in morale.

Final thought in this area: It's really easy to quit when things aren't smooth. Understand that *"gravitational pull"* will always try to get you back to the "easy" way. If you know that in advance and have solutions for the eventuality, you are more likely to keep your commitment and that of your team.

Shoving Them Out of the Nest
You Can Never Fly if You're Stuck in a Tree

I remember raising my children. As I write this, they are both in their mid-twenties, but those youthful years don't seem that long ago. As parents, Barb and I worked diligently to help them gain their education both in school and in the common sense department. In almost every instance where the "common sense" option reared its head, I had some sort of weird flashback to my youth (also seemingly a short time ago). I could hear Mom or Dad in my head extolling the same lessons.

Mindy and Kelli both went out of state to attend universities. By serendipity, they both went to the same area. In fact, they lived together the final full year they were there before moving back. As a parent, I still remember that apprehensive feeling in the pit of my stomach at sending them two thousand four hundred miles away. Mindy was eighteen years old and left as a freshman. Kelli stayed a year at home in a community college before leaving to join her sister in the Pittsburgh area.

In both cases, I clearly remember saying goodbye and driving away. There was that perceptible uneasiness and lump in my throat. I knew that when I got into the car, I was leaving them behind. That just really had never happened for the first nearly two decades. While there were plenty of times they were apart from us for some reason, it was never either too far away or for too long a time. They were always soon to return home. With college, you never know what life will bring and what will influence them. Neither do they, and that's what makes it exciting for them and scary for us! And they call me Mr. Insensitivity. . .

That "shoving out of the nest" was difficult. It was so powerful for me that when both girls came home, we did a little recreation. With Kelli, we were headed to the airport together and stopped off at the hotel I had left her at four years earlier. The university had been using that hotel as a dormitory, and I recalled saying goodbye and not looking back. Kelli is the youngest and that was poignant in its own way. Before bringing her home in 2014, we cheerfully went and took a photo in front of the hotel.

With Mindy, we drove back together over three thousand miles. The final stop before beginning that journey was the dorm I had left her at years earlier. The interesting twist was that we were trying to snap a picture while the current students were moving out! Let's just say that Mindy made me hustle a little to get that picture and take off!

While there is a stark difference between your children and those whom you might coach or mentor, there are certain similarities. The emotion is certainly not anywhere near the same; in fact, you might be looking forward to letting go by the time the send off is ready! However, from a perspective of being a good guide for them, here are a few similarities:

1. **Questions decrease.** When the girls were nearing high school graduation, they were becoming more autonomous. It's one of those things that sneaks up on parents. It can also sneak up on coaches. I know in many of my coaching projects, the number of phone calls and emails at the end are noticeably less than in the beginning. In other words, the protégées have learned and are applying your instruction without your help! That after all, is the goal.

2. **You should know this!** For you parents, do you recall conversations with your teenage kids where you said something like "You know better than that!"? Heck, Barb even says that to me occasionally, which must mean I need more work. There will be times in your coaching and mentoring program where a mentee may ask a question that makes you think, "You should know that." What you want to avoid is enabling them. Often mentees will check their work by asking you even though they know the right answer. It's time to get past that and allow them to occasionally make a mistake and rebound.

3. **The boss knows.** I recall teachers telling me that both girls were capable of handling increased academic workloads and the stress

of moving away from home. They, in a way, were my "boss" in that dynamic. While they genuinely cared, they also took a "30,000-foot view" and could speak with far less emotional attachment. Whoever is the ultimate "boss" overseeing this program, that person may also identify that a transition is needed.

4. **The gut test.** My example here is not my kids but is no less emotional. My mother lived with Barb and me for two years after Dad had died and she was diagnosed with frontal lobe dementia. In the beginning, it made sense. She was fully ambulatory and cognizant of herself and those around her for long stretches. She recognized her friends and us, she was able to feed herself, and she enjoyed much of what life had to offer. What she needed more than anything was companionship. We hired a company to send companions to sit with her, and that worked very well. . .until it didn't. Barb and I knew that a time would come when she either passed away at home or would need to be moved. The daily companions who came to be with her during the day began to prepare us for this by subtly and gently telling us that it was getting to be time.

There was no single event that made us make the decision to move quickly toward transitioning her to a skilled nursing facility. We both just knew at about the same time. I'm guessing Barb knew earlier but allowed me to come to my own gut test in my time. It was really one of those moments where you rapidly go from uncertainty to certainty just from your instincts, which manifest in that weird feeling in the pit of your stomach. Again, this is much more complex than a business coaching program. The similarity is that you will know when your work is done, and it likely will manifest in the pit of your stomach. Your gut feeling tells you it's time to transition. Mom wasn't ready to move herself, yet we knew what was best for her. She had moved beyond our "pay grade." While your mentee or protégée may feel they aren't ready, they probably are.

Bottom line: Have something in place for a smooth transition. That transition might be shifting from coaching to mentoring, or from both to "out of the nest." I am a big proponent of keeping the mentorship going for up to a year. This isn't enabling. It's less work for both mentor and mentee but allows for ongoing support, guidance, and relationship building.

A Captain Jack Extra Point
Holy Crap! It's All About Location. . .

Humans just don't get it. When a dog's got to do his duty, the location means everything. Last night, Dan was taking me on a walk on our regular route. I needed to do my business (#2), and I found one of my normal locations ready and waiting for me. I needed a little extra leash, if you know what I mean. When I have found a potential new spot near the regular, it's very exciting, and my olfactory senses were on fire. On fire!

I needed to turn around a few times on that location to properly lay the groundwork for my task. Dan wasn't making it easy. I was trying to go deeper into the yard; he was impatient and argumentative, exclaiming that I could just go anywhere. Does he just "go" anywhere? No. Neither do I. Location is everything. We somehow managed a compromise and moved on, but it was frustrating for me.

Humans should be worried about location too. Here's what I mean. You need a place you feel comfortable to work, to play, and to exist. These places are where you can relax, and many times, "reset." My favorite Seattle Seahawks player is Russell Wilson (even though he's not much of a barker). He says he has a "reset" place on the field for when things are tough and he needs to start over. We dogs are keen on location. If you humans were too, you'd have a reset location either physically or in your mind. You all need a place to go for peace and inspiration when things are a little tough. It needs to be consistent and always available to you. . . even if you do have to turn around a few times to get comfortable.

We dogs mark our territories so we don't forget. Maybe you should do the same (except in a human way since ours is inappropriate for you).

Just saying. . .

Captain Jack

The Accountability Blueprint

WHERE THE RUBBER GRIPS THE ROAD...

I was a third grader at Olympic View Elementary back in 1973. My good fortune was to be in Mrs. McKinney's class. You see, Mrs. McKinney was the prettiest teacher in the school. I understand that I was nine years old and she was married, but all of that was unimportant. I was in her class and got to spend six hours a day looking at and listening to her. What more could a nine-year-old boy want?

However, another cherished memory of third grade was more essential. Recess. Recess was all about community and the relationships that sprouted from it. For me, it was always about competition. Depending on the season, we were playing football, basketball, baseball, dodgeball, or some other highly spirited game.

One day that December, the usual gang was out on the football field battling in a game that had all the "organizational" ramifications of an NFL playoff game. If you don't think the playground has as much of an organizational structure as any business in this country, just take a few minutes and think back to your own childhood experiences!

Pride was on the line and when you're aiming for that "title" of recess champion, nothing else matters. I was playing wide receiver on offense, and the game was coming to its inevitable conclusion, as we knew the recess bell was quickly approaching. I recall taking off on a fly pattern (that's when the quarterback directs you to run straight down the field as fast as you can while adeptly drawing the route with his finger in the dirt) to attempt to get open and score the winning touchdown. I ran right by my poor pal Galindo, waved my arm frantically in the air, and caught a perfect pass from my quarterback and best friend, Lee. (Lee went on to play quarterback at a Division II school. I'd like to think I helped propel him there.)

I clutched the ball and sprinted into the end zone. I could hear the cheers of the invisible crowd regaling my incredible achievement. And then I lost my mind. Back then there was a football star for the Houston Oilers named Billy "White Shoes" Johnson. "White Shoes" earned his nickname for his brilliant white cleats and his brazen celebration dance. White Shoes would raise his arms triumphantly, get up on his tippy-toes, and flap his legs like chicken wings in triumph. He was the godfather of the touchdown dance. This celebration may have been acceptable in the National Football League, but not here. Galindo wasn't impressed as he inferred that I was mocking him. He approached me and indignantly asked, "Man, what's your deal?"

Of course, haughty with my game-winning play, I was too much in the moment to pay attention to him, so I went to "spike" the ball. Galindo interpreted this as an attempt on my part to punch him. (I wasn't a fighter. I had never punched anyone before that time, and based on Galindo's size advantage to me, would never have dreamed of punching him. My objective was a splendid spike.) Galindo beat me to the punch by hauling off and belting me in the mouth, splitting my lip wide open, resulting in the unavoidable gushing of blood.

Of course, I was fortunate that Mrs. McKinney was there to take care of me. It was an opportunity to recollect that glorious play that had brought us to this point. I walked around with a fat lip the rest of the day. Galindo, visibly shaken over the damage he had wreaked on my face, apologized for his part of the scuffle. We shook hands and quickly went back to being pals. My mother was irate because that night was the Christmas concert at school and I didn't look the part of a choirboy anymore. Of note, I never sounded the part of a singer either, but that was minutia in the grand scheme of things. My mother couldn't care less about the reasons for the fat lip or my inability to sing well. She was more concerned about my appearance.

As third graders, our community response differed from that of the adults. There is an unspoken accountability factor on the playground. Third graders unwittingly carry out accountability by holding those around them to task for transgressions and supporting others in their attempts to succeed (they don't become jaded until sixth grade), chalking mishaps up to serendipity, not taking themselves or others too seriously, and most often, moving forward to the next experience without allowing the past to taint them.

The business world is replete with disasters caused by lack of accountability. Nobody likes being held accountable, and often people will rebel against it. However, the leader who can turn accountability into part of the organizational culture will soon find that both employee morale and positive results will follow.

Defining Accountability
Accountability is a Team Game

We often are advised to be accountable to ourselves. That means we must hold ourselves accountable for our own actions, feelings, words, etc. I'm not here to expunge that definition, just broaden it.

Accountability to one's self is great in theory. However, we humans can be challenged by that very simple philosophy. It isn't normally lack of talent that holds us back from reaching our full potential. The culprit is more personal. . .it's lack of discipline. Lack of discipline is the main culprit for each us in our quest to become better and more significant in our careers. Lack of discipline manifests itself in many ways, including:

- "Cancelling" appointments with ourselves to get important tasks accomplished. We do this with a simple *drag* of the desktop mouse to move it from one day to the next!
- Not keeping self-imposed accountability metrics. Example: I

will exercise for at least thirty minutes for four days every week.

- Not ever starting projects you know are vital out of fear or embarrassment. *What if I fail?*
- Deferring to the easy route rather than the right one. Example: A sales professional who is frightened to call people on the phone, so she chooses to email instead.
- Using time as an ally. *Hey, I've got plenty of time. I will do it next week!*
- No consequences. *Nobody will be angry if it doesn't get done, and I won't discipline myself for inaction.*

Accountability is a "team game," and as a leader in your business or company, it's your duty to help your team become accountable, not only personally but also collectively.

There is no argument that creating accountability partners to accomplish goals is successful. The most common personal example is exercising. For those who have trepidation about going to the gym, having someone to work out with will force them to go so that they don't disappoint or anger their partner. Heck, both people might feel the same way at the same time, yet never speak of it and show up promptly for their workout!

Leadership often entails being a guide and source of direction. Introducing accountability partnerships in your company just might be a great place to set about guiding. Let's discuss what this looks like.

Creating Sustainable Accountability Partnerships

I remember my first accountability partnership. It was 2009, and I was attending my first Alan Weiss event in Providence, RI. It was a workshop designed for fledgling consultants, like myself, and those who might have been around for a while yet hadn't reached their aspirations.

Early on in the workshop, Alan appealed to us to find an accountability partner whom we would use for at least one week after the course. He asked that we accomplish this at the break before lunch so he could explain the rules of engagement for this partnership. There were about thirty-five of us in the workshop. Alan suggested we find someone we didn't know. As you might imagine with a group of expressive consultants, the room came to life at that first break as we all clamored to find our partner.

I quickly found a partner to work with. Laurent and I were contemporaries in age, and we had "seen" each other in Alan's online forum. Laurent was from Montreal, which added an international flavor and curiosity to the association. Alan returned and explained that the minimum requirement for this partnership was that at the conclusion of the workshop, we would meet with our new colleague and share the top three to four things that we wanted to immediately implement pursuant to the class. Alan felt that in order to keep momentum and learning at its best, a quick application of the new material was needed. He said that in one week, we would agree to call each other and hold the other accountable for his or her objectives. After that, we could either continue our partnership or not.

The reasons that this exercise is so vivid are simple. First, it worked. The mere act of making a commitment to somebody else and then having to be culpable is powerful. I use this technique in almost every workshop that I hold for the same reason. Second, Laurent and I not only kept moving forward as accountability partners for the short term, but we kept at it for three years and became good friends. Accountability partnerships normally have a "shelf life" and often need to move on because that accountability can sometimes wane with time and familiarity.

Not many companies that I've run across have a formal accountability program. The reason undoubtedly is that the CEO, president, or leadership team doesn't comprehend its value. I will be as clear as possible right here on the benefits to the individuals and organizations. Then you can determine if it makes sense for your company and/or yourself.

1. **Increased productivity.** When goals and objectives are met because someone is being held to task, performance must go up. Imagine the domino effect when that is multiplied out over an entire organization.

2. **Improved effectiveness.** Doing things poorly more often isn't good. Accountability results in a better product or behavior.

3. **Maximized talent.** Accountability partners draw the most out of each other through encouragement, inspiration, and new ideas.

4. **Reduced risk of "dips."** Malaise invariably hits us all. How long we stay in the valley is the determinant of future productivity. In my experience, the accountability partner is very adept at throwing down the rope to pull you out!

5. **A shared vision.** Goals and objectives are often running on parallel planes. Very often, a shared vision of the future materializes and helps both people.

6. **Advanced skill sets.** You can't help but improve your skills when all the aforementioned things occur. The more skill you have, the more important you are to your company. That applies to leaders and employees alike.

Creating your own internal accountability partnership program is pretty simple. The hard part is sticking to it. Here are my steps and suggestions on how to maximize the process and results.

Step 1: Find a peer who wants accountability. This collaboration needs to be with someone at your level. If you are the boss and want accountability, seek out a colleague at another company to partner with. Not everyone wants to be held accountable. This is a two-way street.

Step 2: Set up a schedule and then keep it. How frequently will you meet? How long will your sessions be? Will you have a proposed end time to see if it's working?

Step 3: Set metrics. How will you know you're meeting your goals? Create some sort of simple tool to keep track of your conversations, your agendas, and your progress.

Step 4: Make commitments at the end of every session. If you are meeting weekly, set a seven-day commitment. If you meet monthly, then it's a thirty-day commitment. Be specific. Example: "I will make five calls within the next week to past clients to see how they are doing."

Step 5: Get started. Don't wait for a perfect time because there won't be one. Just start.

Step 6: Monitor progress. Make sure you are being honest with each other and that you are each benefiting from the interactions.

Step 7: Have fun. Drudgery will never last. This should be fun because you enjoy collaborating with your partner and you are both realizing results.

Dumping Baggage
Ferociously Guarding Your Time and More

One of the perks of being a consultant and speaker is that I get to travel. For some people, travel is a drag. While I do acknowledge there are sometimes misadventures and headaches that accompany traveling (especially by plane), in my view that's the cost of doing business. In my case, "business" is getting to visit and experience new places. In the past three years, I've been to a lot of places across the country, including a 3,004-mile road trip home from Steubenville, OH, to Poulsbo, WA, with my daughter Mindy.

I travel light because I want to be agile and in control. Ninety-five percent of the time, I only carry carry-on. It's uncommon for me not to, and usually involves the requirement of checking something that I can't carry on. I've become a pseudo-expert in packing my bags thanks to one of my great clients. Tom Bihn makes travel bags (among an assortment of bags). Tom designed his bags so that you can pack everything into them and never need to check luggage. He created cool compartments and techniques to load your bags full of all you need. An added feature is the backpack straps that can be tucked away in an outer zipper section when not needed. For me, it's so much easier to carry a bag on my back and keep my hands free. I love the bags because they've improved my ability to travel the way I want to.

My greatest "feat" was packing everything I needed for a one-week, two-city trip in January 2014. Both trips were business-related, so they required the appropriate attire for business casual at the minimum. The first leg was to Miami, where the temperature was a delightful sixty-eight degrees. After three days and two nights there, I jetted off to New Jersey. The entire Northeast was experiencing bitter temperatures. In fact, it was exactly a week before my Seattle Seahawks were to play in MetLife Stadium in East Rutherford, NJ, for Super Bowl XLVIII. When I landed from Miami, it was a balmy nine degrees. To say that I needed polar opposites for clothing was an understatement! This trip required a little more thought and planning than usual due to the changes in the elements. Regardless, I was able to pack everything I needed in one of my Tom Bihn travel bags, hoist it on my shoulders with the backpack straps, and simply carry my briefcase (also a Tom Bihn classic) from airport to airport.

The downsides of checking bags are plentiful—lost or delayed luggage, extra time spent waiting to drop it off and pick it up, unwieldy suitcase sizes making it difficult to move, wheels that never work properly, and more. I also found that when I checked baggage, I usually brought more things that I never used or needed only because I had the extra space. This is a good definition of ineffectual!

Traveling around the country (or the globe, for that matter) is a great metaphor for your life. We are all on a journey and want to experience as much as we can while we are here. We only come around this way once, and we should be focused on maximizing every experience. That means we should be packing light to leave room for the most essential things, plus the important items you pick up along the way!

I've learned over the years that traveling light gives you greater flexibility and agility. It also reduces stress. In order to travel light, you need to make decisions on priorities. As we go through our professional and personal experiences, we pick up lots of baggage. The problem is that many business leaders are hoarders. The danger is that we get so bogged down that it becomes impossible to grow.

This section will help you identify what needs to be thrown off the train by both you and your team. Accountability demands that space be made available for maximizing all aspects of your life, both work and play. Not doing so leads to deleterious results. Much of our excess baggage is self-inflicted, and we've become so attached, we fear losing it. Much like being made to pay an extra premium for baggage being overweight at your airline, you will ultimately pay an extra penalty on your career for carrying around the extra weight. You may even hurt your back!

Time isn't baggage that should be dropped. It's actually a tremendous asset and maybe your most valuable one. Good use of that time will allow you more time to help your team at work and increased discretionary time for you. The result is the ability to maximize your talent and that of others in your world.

Unfortunately, there are bulky and cumbersome weights, which eat up our time and leave less for us. Those are the items that need to be tossed from the train. Freeing up your time by *ferociously guarding* against what takes it up is essential to living a happier and more productive life. ***Are you ferociously guarding your time?***

You protect what you most value. You would certainly agree that we humans would vigorously defend our family, our home, our faith, and our country. We all have prized possessions that we would safeguard. And as many a wealth management expert will encourage you to do, you staunchly guard your money.

Why is it then that we do such a crummy job of guarding what might be one of our most valuable possessions, something that can *never* be recaptured or insured, and something that we all too often complain we don't have enough of? That "possession" is time. I submit to you that if you make ferociously guarding your time a priority, that all your goals, objectives, and dreams will come true both in the short-term and the long run. The good news is that I'm about to tell you how to do it. You just have to have courage, conviction, and discipline.

Why Don't We Guard Our Time Better?

This is an important question to start the process with. I'm certain I've never spoken to anyone who wouldn't agree that time is valuable and feels he or she doesn't have enough of it. Many readily agree they do a poor job of meekly guarding their time, much less being ferocious. So the big question is *why*? If we acknowledge its importance, why can't we do a better job of being ferocious in protecting it? You must be able to answer this question in order to spot the habits of others whom you manage and/or lead. In order to help them, you need to become skilled at identifying bad traits and behaviors.

I propose these four reasons for NOT ferociously guarding time:

I. **No skill acquisition.** Some people lack money skills, which means they are bad at budgeting, saving, and prioritizing how they spend money. Some people suffer from being poor decision-makers. They tend to respond with a knee-jerk reaction, or they get overwhelmed and literally can't make a decision. Just like these two business skills, prioritizing and protecting time is a talent that must be learned, continually improved, and mastered in order to have time to do what you want.

There might exist just over a gazillion books on time management. There is literally no shortage of very good resources to help you learn and understand concepts, techniques, and best practices. I've worked with many clients who have sworn by the works of experts they've read. Yet they also admit they are bad at implementing these concepts. That's because they don't have the skill.

There is a difference between skill and talent. Talent is something you've got within you. Skill is the manifestation and enhancement of that talent to become expert. If you want to be an expert golfer, you spend time out on the practice range and putting green focused on improving skills. If you want to become an artist, you study and practice the skills needed to boost your dexterity with the brush. If you want to master a new language, learn to drive a car, climb rock walls, or play a musical instrument, you must master the skill.

The reason you don't have as much time as you wish is because you are failing to master the skill of prioritizing your time and scheduling. The tools and techniques are out there and you know them. Perhaps the very first priority you need to set and schedule is skill acquisition!

2. **Not a priority.** How ironic that learning how to be better at prioritizing simply falls low on your priority scale! If it were so important, you think you'd have mastered it by now. I speak from experience. Over the span of my life, I've been given numerous books and other really good resources on mastering time management. This happens to everyone in business. I certainly didn't dismiss them. In fact, I knew they would work. My problem is that I just didn't make them a priority. The pain wasn't there. Other things were always more important and consistently pushed aside the time management work like a crazed Black Friday patron on a mission that dispatches all of the window shoppers.

Time management is NOT a sexy topic. Increasing revenue is

the seductive bombshell that always surges to the front when determining the pecking order. What are some other priorities for you? These are the most common activities I hear from executives and leaders I work with:

- Reading and responding to emails.
- Putting out unexpected "fires."
- Dealing with internal "drama" in your company.
- Personal issues that draw you away. (Note that these issues don't have to be negative. In fact, I suggest that the positive "issues" are more likely to distract your attention.)
- Paperwork on the desk. (So much for a paperless world, huh?)
- Not allocating enough time in between meetings (including misjudging travel time).

Let's face it: if you are serious about being better at prioritizing, then you need to start with making it a priority. You must consider this a valuable enough discipline to become proficient in.

3. **To-do list disorder.** I used to live off of "to-do" lists. My lists would become so lengthy and unwieldy, that I was soon overwhelmed. I became adroit at "dragging" the to-dos from one day to the next until they became obsolete or urgent due to my constant postponement of action. Before the days of digital technology, I'd hand write these lists out on various notepads that somehow were kept at divergent locations. The goal was at some point to merge them all together and then prioritize them the next day. This method soon resembled a parking lot at a grocery store around 3:00 p.m. the day before Thanksgiving. In the end, it was an effort in futility. I invested my time in creating this to-do list, only to never use it. This was the ultimate waste of time and effort.

Then digital emerged, and I thought my problems in this area solved. No longer would I need copious notepads kept in various locations only to be poorly tabulated later. It was now all going to happen on my handy-dandy computer. To my dismay, it only got worse! Instead of manually "dragging" activities from day to day, now I was electronically doing it! The results were the same. This time I was just realizing those "results" much faster!

If you are thinking, *Well Dan, that's just bad discipline. All you had to do was do the activities,* you'd be 100 percent right. My problem was that I didn't honor or respect what was on the paper (real or digital). It was *only* a "to-do." Much like Captain Jack Sparrow from *Pirates of the Caribbean* regarded rules as simply "guidelines," I regarded to-dos as drudgery and not as important as a real calendar event. In my experience, this affliction is not unique to me. When I talk with very smart, and often very disciplined, business leaders, they admit to the same trait. It took my work with Alan Weiss to forever change my routine and how I finished my work.

Alan Weiss taught me two critical techniques that I now share with my clients and you. They aren't necessarily earth-shattering, yet require self-discipline to achieve. That being said, they worked for me.

First, I dropped the whole to-do list from my habits. Instead, I took Alan's advice and made everything a calendar event. Instead of being a "guideline" that could be advanced because it wasn't important enough to warrant a real spot on the calendar, I gave it one. It didn't matter if it was simply a callback. . .it got a time. I was better able to manage my day based on how long each activity was going to take. I also became more disciplined on not overbooking myself, which is easy to do. This whole idea of actually using your calendar by applying dates and times to activity has not only benefited me, but the feedback I get from my clients has indicated that when they've adopted the same practice, they've benefited, too. Drop the "to-dos" and get them on your calendar.

Second, I stopped breaking appointments with myself. This is the area that can completely derail the first technique. It was always easy for me to break any "appointment" that was on the calendar with myself. I never had to argue with or persuade myself! From discussions with many people, I've come to the conclusion that breaking appointments, meetings, and dates with one's self is rampant in the business world (and probably in our personal lives as well).

I had to consider myself a client. I wouldn't intentionally break a client meeting. Why would I do that to myself? Because something suddenly came up!

When something suddenly comes up that is deemed more important, we stand ourselves up. Worse, we don't get things done. In order to manage and leverage the baggage you have to its highest use, you must do both techniques concurrently.

4. **Email emergency.** Thirty years ago, I never imagined the concept of electronic mail. I remember one the very first emails I sent. I was working at an insurance agency, and it was about 1995. One of my closest friends, Curt, was in the Navy and out at sea defending our country. Curt sent out an email to many of us to tell us how he was doing and when he planned to be back. Today, this is as common as a peanut butter and jelly sandwich. In 1995, it was really cool.

The email came to me at work (I don't remember having a personal email at that time). I recall walking into my boss's office and asking permission to reply to Curt using my office email. I told Brian that I would cover the cost. Brian chuckled and told me that not only was it fine, but that email had no cost. I was stunned. I thought email was basically the equivalent of Western Union. Free correspondence. . . who knew?

Although it's difficult to quantify methods of communication,

I believe it's safe to say that email is the most used business correspondence among people across the planet. One day, instant messaging and text may overtake it. As of the writing of this book, email remains ubiquitous. So much so that we humans almost can't live without its constant infiltration into our lives. As it's progressed from a desktop service into our mobile devices, the ability to be reached 24/7 anywhere you are has become the norm for all ages. A monster has been created in the staggering amount of "mail" that inundates our lives and our attention. When working with clients, I normally ask them to complete a time journal for a brief, yet significant time to track how they spend their days. Inevitably, email work accounts for an inordinate amount of that time. Believe it or not, you are still in control. The only way email gets a life of its own is if you allow it. If you can control the email avalanche, I promise you that you can regain time. . .and lots of it. You will be dumping baggage!

One of the most common complaints from leaders that I've had the privilege of coaching is that last issue. Email is the enemy that must be fed. Leaders must learn to defeat this enemy AND teach others how to at least tame it. Here are my **5 Best Practices to Email Freedom**:

1. **Lengthen Time Between Email Deliveries.** Many of you have email surging into your inbox about every five minutes, accompanied by the annoying little bell announcing its arrival as if the President of the United States was entering the building. Email is almost never urgent. Truly urgent situations are still dealt with by a phone call. In my family, we will use text for an emergency event, rather than email. I've noted the same from many clients and am counseling business organizations to use the same method for emergency contact with their employees. What this means is that although someone sent something to your email account, it doesn't need immediate attention. It eventually will, but if you look at it when you have appropriated time, it will be

more efficient.

I have set a sixty-minute time frame between emails. You can easily do the same. Read emails when they come up and answer at the same time. More on this technique below, but suffice it to say that if you do this one simple thing, you will be further ahead that you had been.

2. **Avoid Distractions.** If you allow your open door policy to apply while you are reading and responding to emails, you'll wreak havoc on your schedule. Make email management just like any other project. Don't allow someone walking in with their own problem (unless the building is on fire or some other legitimate emergency) hijack your time in dealing with your correspondence.

3. **Reply/Delete/File.** We make this process harder than we need to. Read the email that came in. Make a decision on whether you need to keep it. If you do, file it in the appropriate folder. If not, delete it. If it's spam mark it as such. *Easy peasy.* In addition, if you get newsletters or other digital publications that you no longer want and never read, unsubscribe to them. It's not an insult to the sender. It's just making sure you don't have to take the time to hit "delete" all the time these come through if they no longer pertain to you.

4. **Keep Inbox Clean.** I've been as high as four thousand emails in my inbox, so I know of what I speak. I wish I could say I'm consistently at zero when I end the day because I'm not. However, if you walked into my office and looked at my inbox, it would be under two hundred. I am still working on my goal of one day being "zeroed out" every day. I'm a lot closer than I used to be, and you can be closer too. Here's what it takes to do. . .

Spend fifteen minutes a day by scheduling it on your calendar at a time when you're the least productive. I'm best in the morning and worst in the late afternoon, so that's when I did it.

Go to your inbox and systematically file or delete old "stuff." I found that viewing them by who sent them would allow me to dispatch dozens at a time. Whatever your method, if you spend fifteen minutes a day (while keeping current on ones coming in daily), over the course of time you will get your inbox down to a manageable level. Having too many emails in your inbox is like having a desk overflowing with papers. You can't find what you're looking for and it's distracting to the point of disability at times. Don't overthink this. . .it's easy. Schedule the time, and by working consistently, you will make tremendous progress toward dumping a lot of baggage that's weighing you down.

5. **Manage Your Spam**. I'm not an expert in spam management, and I hate the food by the same name. Figure out how to control your spam as best you can. Unfortunately, I still get a lot of legitimate email stuck in my spam filter and too many that should be junk appearing in my inbox. I don't know how that works, and I'm not going to drive myself crazy with it. Get help from your tech staff, learn online how to deal with it, and implement the best solution for you. My feeling is that nothing will be perfect, so just do the best you can and move on.

If you're like me, it's easy to allow the spam buildup by doing nothing. This past year, I spent a little bit of time trying to make it better, and felt that my time was well invested. You can do the same.

We humans must consistently grow and develop mentally and physically to enjoy a healthy and happy life. In order to do that, we must fiercely guard our time against forces that try to steal it. Many of these forces are actually good causes, appropriate business tools, and well-intentioned people. The time or idea may just not be right for you. This is where you learn to just say NO! There are other "time thieves" that are more insidious because they are often stealthy and masquerade as essentials. You have more control than you think. Choose to spend your time focusing on people and activities that make you better. You can always make another dollar, but you can't make another minute. Be ferocious in guarding those minutes.

If You Need Wheels, You've Packed Too Much

Some final thoughts on the metaphor of traveling through life with the right baggage: My friends at Tom Bihn will suggest that if you have to use luggage with wheels, you've packed too much. As I stated at the outset of this chapter, I've been guilty in the past of packing too much because many of the things I deemed necessary, or thought of as insurance, never were used and just got in the way. My new goal of packing efficiently has made large rolling suitcases extraneous. The results, as I've expressed, have been terrific.

So how do we pack light in our life's journey so we can boldly bolt outside the gate and revel in being Unleashed? Well, allow me to propose five *travel tips* for the rest of your journey:

1. **Pack Essentials First.** Just as you'd pack things like medications and underwear first for a trip, you need to ensure that your most valuable possessions are "packed" first for life. What's essential in your life?
   For me, it's my relationship with my wife and daughters. While I have more friends and family, they are first. It works down from there and others are added, but you need to know where to start. We all will be different. Identification of your essentials is job one.

2. **Go Mobile.** I rarely need to print anything out anymore. All my travel essentials, like airline tickets and hotel reservations, are electronic. I even have transportation covered through services like Uber, so I don't need to carry extra cash.
   Use technology to maximize your opportunities and time. Technology when used for good is a tremendous asset. And it can add quality and comfort to your business and lifestyle.

3. **Roll.** I learned that by rolling clothes, you could maximize

space. This is especially true for suits. Once you start folding, you lose valuable space and end up having to iron.

Roll with the punches. When people or things start to bend, fold, and mutilate your attitude and life balance, things go wrong in a hurry. The time and energy required to "iron out" messes is significant. You can free yourself from this by "rolling with the punches," staying cool and collected, and dispatching anything that needs to be "ironed" in your world.

4. **Don't Bring Extra Things "Just in Case."** As an insurance expert, I may have picked up the bad habit of applying insurance principles to my travel packing. While being safe makes sense with things you can't buy elsewhere (e.g., medicine), it doesn't mean that you have to pack three sets of dress shoes for one black suit. If in doubt, don't take it. If you really need it, you can always buy it later.

I think we all are guilty to a point of packing extras in life too. . .just in case. We humans can pack extra baggage like:
   - Bad experiences
   - Anger and recrimination
   - Preconceived judgments
   - Fear and self-doubt
   - Stress and anxiety
   - Weighty burdens
   - Lofty expectations
   - Guilt

Some of this baggage is based on perceived self-preservation. If we carry this baggage to be ready as excuses for our own failings, then we can look ourselves in the mirror, right? Look, you shouldn't even leave these at home. It's better to just dispose of them for good. You will be better off professionally and personally!

5. **Squeeze and Zip.** Sometimes, you might need to squeeze a little to get that zipper to close. It may leave little room for bringing

anything back with you, but it's always a gratifying feeling to be able to zip your bags closed!

I have found that sometimes I need help squeezing that bag while trying to zip it. Most of us come with two hands, and an extra one can always be "handy." When I'm by myself, it can be much harder and more arduous. I miss that extra hand. We can't expect to traverse this life putting forth our best effort without help. Sometimes that's guidance from coaching and mentoring. Sometimes that's support from family and friends. And sometimes, it's just companionship. If you close yourself off to any of those or other opportunities to advance relationships, you'll never fully achieve your talents or potential. By opening yourself to others, not only will you benefit, but they will too.

A Captain Jack Extra Point
Dog Days of Travel

I don't travel. Dan travels a lot for his business. Occasionally, Bella and I get to go for a "ride." Recently, the ride ends up stopping at the doctor. This is not usually fun for us, and last time, Bella came home with thirty less teeth than she left home with. I'm not really jazzed about taking a "ride" anymore.

I learned that for a dog to travel by air you have to be drugged, get shoved down in some holding area with a bunch of luggage, wake up in some cage that's transporting you somewhere within the bowels of an airport, and finally reunite with your owner in some far off place, now in desperate need of therapy. No thanks! I've watched television and know what happens to your luggage after you give it to the people behind the desk. I'd rather stay at home.

I always know when Dan is leaving because he packs all of his stuff in one or two pieces of luggage. I will say I'm impressed by how much he can squeeze into the bags. He likes to tell everyone he's an expert packer and travels light. I'm not sure what that means, but I think he likes being nimble and fleet of foot. I also know he doesn't give those people his bags!

I don't know why you would want to carry a whole bunch of unneeded luggage and stuff when you travel. For once, I think Dan has it right. By not being weighed down by a lot of extra things, you can enjoy your trip more.

My guess is the same is true about your life. If you don't have the extra weight or the added burden, then you're able to have a lot of extra time and enjoyment in your life. When I go for my walks, I'm burden free (except for the stupid leash). Even when we take those occasional "rides" in the car, I don't have to pack any cares with me. Maybe as you go through your walk of life, you should get rid of anything that doesn't bring value to it. That way, you have room for more of the stuff that does.

Just saying. . .

Captain Jack

Noise

HOW TO DEFY DISTRACTION

Squirrel. That's right. Squirrel.

Captain Jack's biggest distraction in his life is that little furry rodent that scurries about trees, bushes, and open yards. The squirrel is pretty intelligent. He knows that a dog behind a window or on a leash has no chance to nab him. Just like the legendary boxer Muhammad Ali once taunted his opponents, the squirrel gleefully giggles at Captain Jack, driving my canine pal to frenzy.

Captain Jack can spot a squirrel anywhere in the neighborhood with his amazing peripheral vision. If we are on a walk, or if he's merely staring out the window at life, the sudden arrival of a squirrel will divert his attention quicker than a Porsche 918 Spyder going from zero to sixty miles per hour (a scorching 2.2 seconds).

Captain Jack has no keen interest in overcoming his propensity to be distracted when a squirrel enters his life. He believes it is part of his job to guard *his yard* from this most crafty and cunning of enemies. He also has nothing better to do with his time. You do.

I am a good example of how to become distracted. Just ask my wife. Barb could write volumes on my ability to quickly have my attention drawn away from what I was doing when my own "squirrel" enters the picture. That's true in most cases, except when there is a football game on the television.

I've conducted my own self-assessment and concluded that my distractions are pretty simple to identify. My surroundings play a formidable part of distraction for me, so I had to make a very conscious and intentional move to keep my work area as neat as possible. Anyone who worked with me during the sixteen years I was an insurance agent might find this proclamation astounding based on my past office upkeep and maintenance. You are invited to come and view the "new me!"

Extra Point: Let's be honest here. The affliction of being easily distracted is akin to having an addiction. It never really "goes away." It's a daily battle to be focused. I know because it's my malady! There are still many times I whisper (or scream) in my head, *Focus. . .focus.*

Lack of discipline is the enemy of all of us. Distraction isn't the worst vice in the world, yet not being able to control it will mean you will never be able to fully achieve the totality of your talent because something distracted you. Maybe a squirrel. . .

This chapter is titled "Noise." As I've spent the entirety of this opening section discussing distraction, you may come to the conclusion that distraction is a component of "noise." You would be correct, yet there are other factors that fill the "noise bucket." This chapter will focus on defining those and offering solutions to help you work, play, and live in more *silence*. This includes identifying the noise in your world, assessing what can be done to reduce or eliminate it, choosing to what and to whom you should listen, and ensuring that you drop the baggage that no longer is wanted in your life.

Silence of the Bark
Cutting Through the Noise of Distraction

It's time to define "noise." I throw these four components in the "Noise Bucket."

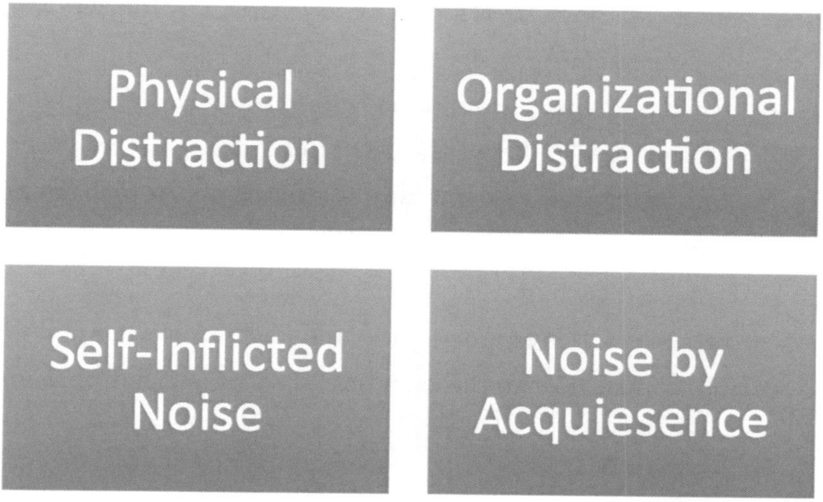

Physical Distraction	Organizational Distraction
Self-Inflicted Noise	**Noise by Acquiesence**

Figure 7.1

Physical Distraction is all the tangible and audible items that come to your view and divert your attention. Here are examples from my own life:

- **Clutter.** This is the squirrel model described earlier in the chapter. Some people can work with a lot of clutter around them. I'm not one of them and my personal view is that in reality, very few of us are. I'm drawn away from the moment by visual stimuli. For example, I might see something on my desk that I remember needs attention (even if I've already accounted for it on my calendar). I don't need a space devoid of all visual objects; however, if it's orderly, the likelihood of my distraction becoming a problem is minimized. What about you? Do visual distractions create a problem with staying on task?

- **Email.** Be honest with yourself—when you see that little visual notification with the *ding* signifying that "you've got mail," it's almost impossible to ignore. Emails are rarely urgent anymore. They've become the de facto method of regular correspondence. We've just made them more important than they really are. In emergencies, people will call you. I've worked with clients who end up spending an inordinate amount of their day simply reading and responding to emails. Do yourself a favor by implementing a very quick Band-Aid (expounded on in the previous chapter): extend the time you receive new emails to at least an hour and have the discipline to keep to that. When it's time for you to see them, deal with each one at that moment. This will keep your mind free from that noise and your inbox clean and current.

- **Talk radio.** I love sports radio and listen to it when I'm driving in the car. I simply can't have it on as a backdrop to my work at my desk, whether it is working on a project, writing a column, or strategizing. I'm distracted by the topic being discussed. That being said, there is research that shows that we can be very effective with a little background noise. As I'm typing this chapter, I've got Pandora on the Glenn Miller Orchestra station and I'm listening to *Rhapsody in Blue*. This station is primarily instrumental, so it actually adds a rhythm to my work without being distracting.

- **Television.** I have colleagues that actually have a television on in their office while they work. Most times, the program is news, finance, or business related. I give them credit because, just like with talk radio stations, I get preoccupied with the content on the TV and lose focus on what I'm doing. Interestingly enough, I do get notices of breaking news on email and mobile phone notifications. Important events that do require your attention can always reach you in our digital and "real-time" world. Just make sure that not every notification becomes "urgent" to you!

Organizational Distraction is something that no one is immune to. If you work in an office or any other location where other people are present, you are exposed to a lot of stimuli—it's the old water cooler principle. You are either part of or privy to conversations from other people on their personal lives (both good and bad). You hear about their children and grandchildren, complaints about work and family, the latest happenings on last night's reality TV show, the results from the big game over the weekend, and a myriad of other trivial experiences. While a good personal relationship between coworkers is healthy and often essential to building your team chemistry, you would agree that there is always a time and a place. There is plenty of research showing that employees (and very often, employers) engage in a disproportionate amount of gossip and drama during business hours.

As the leader of your business, you need to ask some important questions. First, are *you* part of the problem? Do you take part in actively engaging others so that you are not only distracting them, but also consenting to their behavior? The other area where you might have culpability is if your behavior and leadership style is the topic of conversation! Effective leaders rarely have people discussing their merits around that water cooler; however, the inadequate leader will find that angst and bitterness will spread like a wildfire in August.

This book will offer a lot of ideas to help you become the best possible leader. While there is much you can control, and many things you simply can't, the normal day-to-day work environment needs balance. I worked for years in an office environment. When I began working from home in 2005, I saw major increase in my own productivity. There was nobody there to be interrupted by, no conversation to distract me, and nobody for me to interrupt. Finding your organizational balance comes down to your own quality control methods and communications.

Self-Inflicted Noise is just exactly what it sounds like. It's the battle within your own head. You're familiar with the humorous scene played out on a poor sap's shoulders between the good and the evil selves. On one side, you have your doppelgänger with red horns, red cape, and crimson pitchfork telling you to make one decision. On the other shoulder is perched the angelic you, who is often more prudent and thoughtful. In my experience, both sides will engage in a raging verbal battle that goes right through your head.

Here's the deal: both apparitions often have good ideas, and weighing pros and cons is fine. The challenge comes when the noise in your head turns negative and mean-spirited. The most troubling aspect of this is that as a leader, you wouldn't dream of saying the things you say to yourself to others because you'd either be losing employees or being sued for creating a hostile work environment.

As a lifelong practicing Catholic, I take part in the sacrament of reconciliation two to three times per year. That's what everyone else simply calls "going to confession." Not everyone likes going to confession, and many a Catholic has left the church for this reason. I don't like it either, yet I've found it to be an important self-assessment tool. An antecedent of entering the small room where you will confess your offenses to a priest is an *examination of conscience*. A few years ago, I added a mobile application for confession that includes a checklist using the Ten Commandments as a guide to examining exactly what your sins might be. I found this archive very demanding, yet exactly what I needed because it focused me on self-assessment.

The examination of conscience takes me less than ten minutes to complete, but it forces me to be blunt with myself. I will find behaviors that I don't care for that involve my own choices and priorities, which I have full control over. In a sense, I'm guilty of self-inflicted wounds. The same process can be done in a professional examination of conscience.

What noise are you guilty of inflicting on yourself? Give an honest assessment of this. Use my professional examination of conscience to exorcise your internal business demons:

Figure 7.2

Do you berate yourself?	Do you lack confidence?	Do you fear failure?
Do you feel inadequate?	Do you give up too easily?	Do you fear what others think of you?
Do you fear rejection?	Do you call yourself names?	Do you talk yourself out of taking risks?

All of these questions point to the main problem of lack of self-worth and lack of confidence. This concept has been constant in the book and will continue to be so, as it's a serious obstacle to your becoming Unleashed. Just as it takes a high level of fortitude to complete a self-assessment like this, it also requires a strong discipline to overcome your noise. This is the first step.

The next step is also similar to going to confession. Once my confession is complete, the priest will assign me "homework." We call it our *penance*, and it normally involves a mixture of recitations of prayers and other actions to help us to focus on right behavior and cast aside the bad habits. Once you're done with this examination of conscience I've provided, I suggest you find someone in your business world to "confess" to. This is often a business coach or mentor, a person in your organization whom you trust can help you, or a trusted colleague who can hold you accountable. Confess your self-inflicted sins and ask for your own "homework" to cast aside that stinking thinking and improve your self-worth and confidence to become *Unleashed*.

Noise by Acquiescence is perhaps the most ominous. We all have chosen willingly (or unwillingly) to put ourselves in projects, situations, and commitments that add "agitation" to our world, even when we aren't immediately involved in them.

In 2009, I threw my hat in the ring to replace a school board director who was forced to resign due to health reasons. I was selected over two other candidates and accepted the remainder of his two-year term. At the end of that time, I chose to run for the same office for another four years.

School boards are volunteer organizations created to make policies, handle budgets, and oversee the entire operation of a school district. In this case, this was a district that had a $60 million budget and over one thousand employees. It was basically a complex small business with a lot of rules and regulations governed by the state. As elected public officials, we also became subject to a diverse group of "investors." We were obliged to listen to the analysis of the community and the seemingly endless complaints that came from that analysis. I thought I knew going in that this role would have its share of "politics." I had no idea how much.

Without diving too deeply into minutiae that you don't care about, suffice it to say that in mid-2013, a group of what I will call "angry and bitter" parents erupted onto the scene. They became the proverbial "thorn in the side" for the board and the administration. They created a constant negativity and were relentless in their quest to be adversarial and destructive to the administrative and strategic process of running the business of a school district. This group, in combination with other internal factors, had relegated this "job" to an "unwanted chore." By September 2014, I needed to make a decision.

I concluded that the light at the end of the tunnel was actually an oncoming train. I abhorred opening my school board email daily, hated going to meetings, and what was once a rewarding position had become a major distraction in both my professional and personal life. The negativity and avarice caused by this small group was making me *angry*. This anger transcended time so that it invaded my workday, my time with family, and my thoughts. When it got to the point that I was looking forward to December 2015 (the end of my elected term) and it wasn't even December 2014 yet, that signaled a time to "fish or cut bait."

That was when I got some very fine "coaching" from Barb. She inquired, "What if you had a client come to you with this issue? What would you tell them?" My response was, "I would tell them to resign and move on with their life." BAM! Point taken.

I made the decision and acted on it within twenty-four hours. Outside of a week of answering questions and dealing with the fallout, the quality of my life had been ameliorated exponentially. It wasn't so much the time being spent in meetings that was the difference. It was the removal of the *distraction* that had become a constant companion in my head. This distraction wasn't going to go away organically, so it had to be vanquished.

For too long, I had acquiesced to this "noise." The noise was constant, negative, and unrelenting. By accepting it past a point of trying to change it, I was allowing something clearly in my control to adversely affect everything else I cared about. Fortunately, I came to that realization before any further "damage" to my time, to my business, and to my good mental health happened!

What about you? Is there something in your life that is no longer fun, no longer rewarding, or now a detestable activity that you should take a strong and honest look at?

Here's what you do if the answer is yes: No matter how hard it is to break away from this activity, you've got to do it, or the excess noise it creates in your life will only intensify. This is particularly true if this is a volunteer position. Life's too short, and you have too much on your plate, to add second and third helpings. Almost all activities have a shelf life and eventually run their course. I've seen too many situations where people have hung on for too long because the role had defined them, or because of some other self-serving reason, including perceived power. As a business leader, you can set a good example for your people. You can also add vibrancy and space to your life, even if it's simply time for yourself.

Transferring Techniques
How to Teach Others to Be in Silence

We always start with you, and that's what we've done in this chapter. This is a leadership book, and so we need to talk about how you can lead most effectively to maximize the talents and skills of those around you to the benefit of all. Once you've donned your own oxygen mask, it's time to help others.

The good part is that the strategies, concepts, tactics, and practices that it took for you will be the same that you can teach to others. The hard part is that, many times, your key employees, your managers, and your direct reports don't have the desire to change, nor even see the need to. That's where being influential comes in to play.

Transferring your knowledge and assistance takes a bit of its own strategic planning. Let's simplify the process and break it down into five parts:

Figure 7.3

Observe isn't as easy as it sounds. Merely looking and watching won't always give you the information you need. You must know what you're looking for.

Signs that the noise is becoming a distraction and a detriment to others include:

- Reduced level of productivity (especially that which can be measured)

- Lateness in responding to voice mails and emails
- Always working late or coming in early to get work done. Be careful with this one as there may be other legitimate factors (e.g., diminished staff, an unusually busy period of time, or poor planning on your part)
- Others telling you (make sure this comes from people with only best interests at heart)
- Signs of stress and anxiety
- Pile of work grows and grows
- Increased mistakes
- New undesirable behaviors (e.g., tardiness, short-temperedness, obvious distraction, etc.)

When I coached basketball, I used to video record all the games and some of the practice sessions. I would watch the recordings first, identify areas of both strength and weakness, and then re-watch them with my players. Getting teenage girls to focus on using video as a tool for improvement can be a challenge. Most often, they used video as a tool for seeing how their hair looked. That being said, I always got their attention when pointing out flaws with the admonishment that "the video never lies."

Observation is critical for a lot of reasons; it's imperative to help keep tabs on what's going on in your company. I constantly advise my clients to deal with issues based on "observed behaviors." Just like game film in sports, "the video doesn't lie." In your case, your memory and observed behaviors don't lie. You should record and keep them for future use. You can then go on to the next step of the process.

Analyze is the part of the process where you try to understand whether what you observed makes sense. For instance, employees telling you of the faults and failures of others may just be the result of jealousy or sour grapes. On the other hand, they might be giving you a very accurate picture of a situation you weren't aware of. An Unleashed leader needs to be able to step back and assess, rather than jumping to conclusions. I believe there is more "art" than "science" to analysis in a leadership situation. Your experiences and intuitiveness will almost always be a good guides. The key thing here is to not always expect a worst-case scenario. Be ready to give the benefit of the doubt to a person, account for lapses in judgment and decision-making, or chalk up a one-time event to serendipity. Once you've observed and analyzed, you're ready to move on to the next step.

Offer suggestions for improvement and encouragement. You're likely in a position of influence, so your offer will at least be listened to. While I would certainly like to add raising teenagers to this concept, I think I will have to pass!

Offering advice and suggestions doesn't correlate with being autocratic. While the some change of actions and behaviors might be required, the tone of the offered instructions doesn't have to be demanding. I'm not suggesting being weak in your coaching. What I do encourage you to be is, well, encouraging. The best leaders know how to use influence and language to incite change. The offer to help is far more powerful than the demand to change.

Monitor means you hold your team members accountable to the changes. This doesn't include brow-beating, hovering, or micromanaging them to the state of paranoia. It also requires that you don't forget about them! Have you ever given out suggestions or advice and not seen them completed after an initial start? It's human nature to assume that the other person didn't care or wasn't listening. The more practical theory is that they fell back into comfortable habits because their mentor didn't care enough to help them continue with their momentum.

Monitoring change is, in my opinion, the most important step in any change management, whether it's personal behavior or improving a business process. For leaders, it's easy to let things slip by because you think the hard work is done. In reality, the hard work is making sure the implementation stuck!

Help is an offshoot of monitoring. If you observe (see how this is a circular process?) that changes to behaviors, activities, and processes are stalling, offer your help. I can't recall off the top of my head any significant changes in my life that were successful immediately. They all required some level of perseverance, patience, and ongoing support.

The need for help doesn't imply that a person is slow to grasp concepts or unwilling to change. What is does mean is that in order to continually build a culture of teamwork, improve morale, and effect important change, you have to always be willing to step in and help those who need it, whether they know they do or not.

To Whom Are You Listening to and Why?
Techniques for Reducing Unsolicited Advice

Blondie was our first family dog. She was a small, totally white, terrier mixed breed. Her given name was perfect as it affirmed her platinum white appearance. As new dog owners, Barb and I decided that we should enroll Blondie (and us) in dog training classes. Because my schedule best fit the night classes, and because Barb thought some of this training might rub off on me, I was the chosen dog leader.

The class "dog whisperer" was a petite but powerful lady named Gail. Gail owned and professionally trained Dobermans. For all of her lack of stature and her friendliness to us humans, she was one tough drill sergeant who could make any Marine at boot camp think twice about crossing her.

One of the things she taught us was that our dog needed to recognize and respond to our voice. We had this exercise where all the dogs would be placed in a small space centrally located in the room. All the owners would hide out of sight. The first trick was to get most of the dogs to stay in that circle until they were called!

When Gail was ready, she would call out the name of a dog and the human trainee would reenter and call for the dog to come. The point of this lesson was not only to have the dog come on command, but also to teach the other dogs to respond to only their personal masters. These dogs eventually came to take orders from only their humans. In other words, they didn't accept unsolicited advice from others; they stuck with their mentors.

If you are like most humans, you get advice from many sources. I'm willing to wager that about 75 percent of it is unsolicited. Here are some examples:

- The person who approaches you and asks if they can give you advice on your makeup or the style of suit you are wearing.
- The employees who offer you advice on how to fix an organizational problem, when the sole beneficiary is them and their agenda.
- The person who has just heard you give a presentation and wants to offer suggestions on how to improve your public speaking chops.
- The customer who has recommendations on how to improve your store's appearance.
- The blogger who offers sage counsel on the inaccuracies of your most recent publication.
- The client who knows how to manufacture your product better.
- The neighbor who has opinions on the best school for your child to apply to.
- The social media mafia that inundates you with products to help you lose weight, savvy opinions on whom to vote for; and instructions on how to live your life.

You can't help but hear this incessant noise. And many of you succumb to it. One person out of a thousand employees has a complaint, and you take it to heart. One person thinks you should behave differently, and now you think you might need to. One article on social media informs you that milk will kill you and you children, so you remove it from your refrigerator and your diet.

You need to be punctilious about whom you listen to and why. People who offer unsolicited advice, even in seemingly the most amiable manner, do it for their sake, not yours. They often simply want to hear themselves talk, appear to be an expert, or desire the adulation of you and all those within earshot.

This concept might seem clear on the surface, but it's not. I've given you some examples of unsolicited advice, so now let me provide some personal examples of "solicited advice," so you will be able to identify them in your world.

My wife has total immunity. We've been married nearly thirty years, and I plan on keeping that streak going, so I accept her advice in any matter! That being said, she's never offered it in any area where she didn't have some level of expertise. She can at any time inform me that my clothes don't match, and I will immediately change. She's never attempted to offer opinions on how I should consult or how to swing a golf club. I trust her because I know she genuinely has my best interest at heart.

My **Toastmasters club members** have free reign to advise me on speaking. I have the right to accept or reject their advice; however, by dint of my accepting membership and attending meetings and speaking, I've given them authority to speak freely.

I am part of a great **group of colleagues** in my global consulting community. When I post questions on the online forums, I've opened myself up for advice. When I've collaborated in mastermind groups, I've allowed them to call me out when I need it. In essence, I've joined these associations with certain people because I trust their wisdom and intentions.

My hired **coaches and mentors** get free reign too. I've used the services of many of them over the past decade. They've been hired, not to be my "friend" but to be bluntly honest to help me improve.

These are just four examples. I have other family, friends, colleagues, and clients who fall into this august and exclusive circle for me. At some level, I've vetted their expertise, wisdom, intent, and perspicacity. Like Blondie did for me as her "leader," I intentionally ignore the rest.

Listening to the wrong people can be ruinous to your health and your ability to lead. You will clog your brain with too many negative, and often wrong, thoughts; your confidence may be shaken; and your desire to please everyone will paralyze you. As I said earlier, you must be very careful about whom you take your solicited advice from.

Consider this my list of people and groups that you can scrutinize as potential advisers. Note that there will be caveats for many, and you should always be wary about intent and agenda. I don't propose that you are overly judicious to the point of absurdity. What I do submit is that you develop allegiances and understandings with others, both professionally and personally, and monitor them to ensure that everyone wins.

1. **Spouse or Significant Other.** All relationships have varying degrees of stability. I've been blessed by having a very good one for my life. If you have one, then your significant other is your ultimate trusted adviser.

2. **Family with a BIG Caveat.** Your adult children are hopefully going to be trusted advisers in many areas. In my life, I know where I can find good medical and fashion opinions! Not everyone in your family will have the same coziness. Most families will have members that offer advice just to be heard or to be contrary. You need to seek out those whom you trust with their wisdom and discreetly tune out the rest.

3. **Professional Organizations.** I mentioned Toastmasters and mastermind groups. For many executives, memberships in Vistage and Excell (and like organizations) offer superb peers to help them when they need it.

4. **Accountability Partners.** We've discussed accountability partners already in this book. This is a given. If you trust them enough to enter into this professional relationship, then you should trust their judgment in giving you feedback.

5. **Coaches and Mentors.** I saved this one for last. In this case, you're paying for solicited advice. You hired this person for a reason. Trust them to have your best interest in what they tell you.

One final note on this topic: In my experience, those that are the BEST solicited advisers never offer unsolicited advice. You have usually sought them out for some reason. If you encounter someone who is always offering you their advice and you never asked for it, they probably aren't a good fit for an adviser. However, if through your relationships, research, and other business dealings, you find someone who offers sage advice and you want to learn more about how this person can help you, then that is the sign of a good prospective partner.

Creating Your Own Bark
How to Rise Above the Clatter

My observation is that dogs don't have a lot of wasted energy. They expend what they need to in order to get the desired results. We humans tend to think we must "overwork" ourselves in order to be viewed as "successful."

I recall one of my bosses (and good friends), Brian, telling me about an encounter he had with a young man on the beaches of Greece back in the mid-1990s. He was on the trip with his wife courtesy of one of his insurance company partners. Brian was hanging out on the beach and came across a young man selling food and beverages from a small food truck he owned. Through some conversation, Brian found that this guy was an American and had a business degree from a prestigious university back in the United States. Brian expressed his surprise that a young man with such credentials was peddling iced mochas and sandwiches on a beach, rather than climbing the corporate ladder back home.

The young man's response made an impression on Brian, and on me as I heard it. He said that he had done the corporate thing for a while and felt the normal stress and pressure that comes with it. He found himself in Greece somehow and ended up buying the food truck and camping out on a bustling beach full of tourists with fat wallets.

He said, "You guys work too hard. You put in crazy hours to pay for ultra-expensive homes and toys. You end up so tired, stressed out, and sad that you can't even enjoy what that hard work and money bought." He continued, "I started this business because it's fun and has zero stress. I make enough money from it to support a good lifestyle, and I spend my days in the sun on a beach in Greece. Who has it better, you or me?"

This guy created his own, unique "bark." He chose to eschew the corporate world (probably the smart play) for his own lifestyle, schlepping food out of a truck on the beaches in Greece.

You can also create your own bark around your leadership style. It shouldn't mimic anyone else, no matter how successful they are or were. Just like our food truck dude created his own lifestyle, you must create your own, unique leadership style.

A Captain Jack Extra Point
Sirius Teaching Lessons

Dan was telling me that one of the big issues he is working on with the school board is having dogs in the classroom. I guess there are some dogs called "therapy dogs" that come and help kids learn in the classroom. Me. . . I can't do it. These dogs have to be on their best behavior all the time, be docile, not chase squirrels, and teach kids. I can't do any of the first three, and what I can teach kids. . . their parents want no part of, believe me!

Here's what I would teach:

- *Take risks. Fail. Learn. Take more risks. Dogs would never have any fun if we didn't take our share of risks. Humans can have that same level of fun by taking risks too. While I know there are human risk-takers out there (I've seen the people jumping off cliffs and out of airplanes), I know there are boardrooms and cubicles filled with humans not thinking risks are worthy of taking.*

- *Get lots of sleep. Dog brains need lots of sleep, and so do humans from what I understand. Humans work too hard sometimes. Get more sleep.*

- *Learn how to influence. I influence Dan all the time to feed me, take me out for a walk or other unmentionables, watch TV, and let me sleep on the bed. We dogs influence with our eyes and natural charm. Humans use language.*

- *Find new adventures in the same old yard. My yard is my regular stomping grounds. Other dogs have fenced yards. Either way, we see the same thing every day, but we make each day a new adventure. Humans get discouraged too easily. Just because it's the same yard, doesn't mean you can't keep having fun. Find new smells!*

- *Live in the moment. Sometimes I get in trouble, but I forget about it and move on. Humans tend to mope about bad things too much, and then the bad things linger on longer than they ever should have.*

You see some dogs can provide therapy, and some might just need it themselves. I think I may just fall into the latter category, but who cares. I'm having fun!

Just saying. . .

Captain Jack

The Entrepreneurial Attitude

IN SEARCH OF ACCOUNTABILITY AND LOYALTY THROUGH MOTIVATION

When I was growing up in the 1970s, the education system was preaching one main destination for its students. It went something like this:

- Learn as much as you can in twelve years of school
- Find out what you're good at (not necessarily what you LIKE)
- Go to college and get a degree
- Go work for a company that will take care of you for thirty to forty years to earn enough to retire comfortably, and
- Retire with a white picket fence and relax. (Note that not much has changed in the present day education field, which is part of the overall problem.)

That's pretty much what my father did. This wasn't necessarily a bad thing in those days. He spent thirty years with one employer (the United States Navy) and then another eighteen years with another (Oak Harbor School District). Some would argue that this concept worked as it put me through college and made a very comfortable life for my parents. It's almost impossible to argue that point. Dad did what he felt he had to for his family, even though he didn't like his last job. I'm grateful because had we moved, or done anything differently, I would not have met my future wife and raised the family that I did. Dad was a hero in that regard.

Dad loved the Navy, so spending thirty years there was the right thing for him. Had he been allowed to stay forever, he gladly would have. In 1973, he retired at the age of forty-eight. We lived in a lovely little spot on Whidbey Island (northwest about one hundred miles from Seattle) in a city called Oak Harbor. Oak Harbor was a relatively small community with limited job opportunities, especially in 1973. Dad had a GED because he left high school early in 1942 to enter World War II. In his thirty years in the Navy, he learned a great deal as an administrator and excelled in that field. He loved research, process, and everything that was involved with administrative and management functions. He would have made a terrific business administrator.

Dad actively searched for jobs even before he officially retired. He tried a variety of businesses and was continually told he was "over-qualified." Executives and business owners all told him that due to his high level of skill, they were afraid to hire him and then have him leave for greener pastures later when he found a job that more suited his expertise. Dad did his best to allay those fears and promised that wouldn't happen. If these people had only known Dad and his intense sense of loyalty, they would have hired him in a second. But they didn't, and Dad started getting nervous. He had done some job seeking in Seattle, and there were several opportunities in the big city. However, that's when his loyalty kicked in. Nobody else in the Weedin family (Mom, my maternal grandfather, and me) wanted to leave Oak Harbor. We had made a home, grown roots, and were happy. Dad decided against accepting office jobs with decent pay to remain in Oak Harbor. I don't know if I could have done that.

Our next-door neighbor was the assistant superintendent of public schools for Oak Harbor. He knew of a custodial position coming up at the junior high. It paid very little, was terribly laborious (especially for a guy pushing fifty) and meant night hours at the start. But it was a job, and Dad took it. He stayed for eighteen years until he finally retired for the last time.

That job became Dad's "yard." It was comfortable because it meant a steady paycheck and benefits. Though he never said it, I've always believed the job search Dad had in 1973 soured him on the prospects of ever doing it again. I think deep down he feared that there was nothing better that he could do and sacrificing his pride and his body was easier than the alternative of looking for something that better matched his talents. He didn't care for the job at all. It was grueling work and he often didn't receive the respect he deserved. He did it for us, and as I stated previously, I'm eternally grateful. Yet, I often wonder how deeply the pain of not being able to reach out and do more was there for him during those last nearly two decades of his "career."

Here's what this story means for you. My dad wasn't wired to be an entrepreneur in the true sense of the word. He was happier working for someone else and doing a good job. While he was loyal, the job had more to do with getting a paycheck than the reward he gained from it.

A postscript on Dad's story is worthwhile here. Dad became somewhat of a legend in his last five to six years as a custodian at Crescent Harbor Elementary. By that time, he was a regular on the day shift and worked while school was in session. Dad loved kids, and they were fond of him. As computers started coming into vogue in the 1980s, the teachers started using Dad to help the students. The kids would write creative stories, turn them in to Dad, and he would transfer them onto the class computer. He would not only type them in, but he would help the students with their grammar and punctuation and encourage them in their work. Before long, all the teachers were asking him to help. I still remember the tremendous amount of gratitude the staff and administration of the school had for him. He even kept doing this for years after he retired as he would come in to volunteer in the classrooms. This was the point where he basically started "playing" for someone other than his family, and it elevated his work experience. He was significant to others and all of a sudden had buy-in. He became entrepreneurial.

How do you create that spirit in your team right now? Regardless of where your employees are in their careers, can you enhance that entrepreneurial spirit within them to ensure they aren't merely punching a clock for a paycheck, but have buy-in for their careers and being significant to others? This chapter will explore this concept in more depth.

What's in It for Me?
Creating a Sense of Ownership

An *entrepreneur* is defined in the dictionary as, "A person who organizes and manages any enterprise, especially a business, usually with considerable *initiative* and *risk*." The two italicized words are significant.

I started my consulting practice in 2005. At the time, I was forty years old and had two kids in high school with college staring us right in the face. I had been working in my craft for almost eighteen years and at my current employer for ten of those. I was comfortable in my pay and position. It offered security and flexibility, with a lifestyle that was all but assured with continuing effort. The problem was that I wasn't happy and was seeking more. I had an entrepreneurial spirit that was burning inside of me and ready to be Unleashed. In order to become an entrepreneur, what needed to be ignited was initiative and risk tolerance.

Initiative is action. How many dogs do you see sitting at the edge of an open gate with no action or movement? Probably the only ones are old, tired, and deeply unmotivated! Many a human has had terrific ideas with no initiative to back them up. My initiative was simple. Do research. Talk to the family. Tell my employer. In that order. Short and sweet sentences that all required big action. Without going into detail on each, the message here is that without action at every step, the "big idea" is going to die. How many wannabe entrepreneurs never made it because the journey ended with inaction?

Risk is required every day by every one of us. We each take a risk getting out of bed and performing tasks and activity in and out of the home. Driving a car may be our biggest risk, yet most of us accept the exposure even though we don't have full control of all the hazards. We have a high *risk tolerance*. Entrepreneurs take on risk when they acknowledge that their big idea may just fail miserably, cost them a lot of money, damage relationships, and/or open them up for lawsuits. Many people don't have the tolerance for that risk, yet entrepreneurs do. This isn't a judgment or value statement; it's simply how people are wired.

Creating a "sense of ownership" in employees must be a leadership objective. What a leader wants to inspire through the culture of the organization is employees caring as much about the success and significance of the business as the owner does. When leaders fail to create this mindset in employees, they get people trading time for money in the form of a paycheck. When they are successful, however, the results look a lot like what you might define as a deep loyalty, a healthy respect, and a sense that the company belongs to employees too.

People examine initiative and risk around one basic principle: "What's in it for me?" What was in it for me were these important *personal* factors: keeping all the money that I earned, being the sole decision-maker for my future, greater autonomy and flexibility, personal pride and accomplishment, and the ability to be nimble and to shift without regard to someone else's agenda. That was me. What are yours?

Extra Point: If you're an entrepreneur, small business owner, or CEO/president, why did you take the initiative and risk? Take a few minutes right now before moving on with this chapter to self-assess. Write the answers down if you must. What was in it for you? Are those reasons *still* the same? If they aren't, have you been able to shift?

All initiatives have personal objectives. In order to get your employees and team to have an entrepreneurial spirit within your company, you need to find out what motivates them. . .what's in it for them.

Beyond the Pay Stub
Engendering Loyalty and Buy-in

This is what I call thinking "beyond the pay stub." Your employees may not have the risk tolerance to start their own company and that's fine. In order to make business work, we need diversity—the risk-takers, the skilled technicians, the able workers, and the strong support team. That being said, everyone has that personal objective, as I stated in the previous paragraph. It's your job to figure out what makes your team members tick, and how to leverage that in a positive way for them, for you, and for your clients.

Extra Point: As I am writing this chapter, I am reminded of a particular client and his sales team. Keith inquired at one point about my intentional language around the person who buys our services. I call them clients; he called them customers. Here is the difference: customers see you as a vendor. Customers buy groceries, batteries, appliances, landscaping supplies, and ice cream to name just a very few things. They often compare prices and simplicity of purchase. Clients see you as an adviser and someone they can't do without. Clients are provided value by consultants, experts, doctors, CPAs, attorneys, and web designers. If you want to create *stickiness* in your client relationships, shift your language and that of your sales and customer service team. Heck, change it organizationally! That's what Keith did. He used to sell lumber products to "customers." He now sells to "clients." What about you?

I've worked with countless business owners and talked with even larger numbers of employees over nearly three decades of my career. Here are the five most common factors that earn thinking "beyond the pay stub" for employees.

- **Secured Lifestyle.** It's not necessarily about the amount of money, but that the money will be consistent to ensure a desired lifestyle for the remainder of your employees' lives. While many owners think employees only care about money and increasing income, most of their employees really want a fair wage based on their contributions to the company. They also want to know you will stay in business long enough for them to pull it out!

- **Appreciation.** People crave respect and the sense of being part of something bigger than just themselves. Don't assume that they don't want to hear it regularly. While the squeaky wheels are getting your attention, your shiny ones are being ignored.

- **Safe and Fun Work Environment.** That means your employees feel confident you are doing everything you can to send them home in the same physical condition as when they came in. It means that they aren't forced to listen to toxic personalities being constantly negative. It means being able to smile and enjoy their labors. It means collaboration and fellowship. And it means community.

- **Chance to Grow.** This isn't exclusive to income. While we all want that, your employees also desire the opportunity to improve their talents, learn new skills, be challenged, teach others, and be intellectually and professionally stimulated.

- **Pride.** Have you ever been to a family function and had to endure the wailing, lamenting, and gnashing of teeth of family members' work woes? We all have and maybe even have been the *giver* of the woe! While it's very easy to label these people as complainers, the reality is that they are dissatisfied for some reason and that culpability falls at least equally on the employer. I acknowledge that some people exist in a scarcity mentality, yet I also know that most simply want to be proud of where and whom they work for.

So how do you engender that loyalty? Now is the time to look back and review the five factors just mentioned. If you focus on these, you will be well on your way. However, just looking without doing accomplishes nothing. Just like the two components of entrepreneurship—initiative and risk—you need to apply both looking and doing to this process.

    1. **Ask questions.** Seek out what motivates your people and find

trends. Be in the moment and open to whatever they say.

2. **Think fun.** That's right, fun. We all want to earn increasing revenue and cut out expenses, but it's much easier to do both when everyone enjoys what they are doing!

3. **Collaborate.** You can mix this in with fun by creating activities and exercises designed to learn more about your team.

4. **Be vulnerable.** That's often tough for leaders to do. I find this can actually be a generational thing as well. Women do this better than men, and it's often been an asset for them. Being vulnerable isn't equivalent to being weak. To the contrary, it's a strong leader who can admit failings to help others learn and grow.

5. **Put people first.** That's an easy axiom to slap on your business cards and boardroom, but it's much tougher in action. We can easily forget trials and tribulations that employees are facing. Kindness, generosity, and smiles go a long way. You will be an effective and admired leader when you exhibit true servant leadership.

From Garage Band to Rock Star
Building Superstars

In July 2013, Barb and I went to see Paul McCartney perform a concert at Safeco Field. At the time, McCartney was seventy-one years old, and I was figuring this might be my last chance to see a former member of the Beatles in person. It turned out to be the best concert I've ever seen. Sir Paul went for over three hours without a break (including two encore performances featuring the remaining members of legendary local band, Nirvana) to the delight of a packed house. It was a spectacular event that I will always remember.

Prior to the concert starting, Barb and I went into the club area to get a beer and wine. As we were waiting in line, a guy, perhaps in his mid-sixties, walked by. He had gray hair pulled back into a ponytail and was wearing a black AC/DC shirt and jeans. He appeared to like an occasional beer or two as his midsection protruded ever so slightly in his vintage concert shirt. A few minutes later, I saw Barb vigorously texting and smiling. I asked, "What are you doing?" Barb responded, "I'm texting the girls about the guy that just walked by and you." She now had my attention (especially due to the smirk still visible on her face). She handed me her phone and said, "Read my text. . ."

I've seen the future with your dad, and it's not pretty!

Of course, they all know me well and laughed at my expense. She's probably right. My love of rock music and my flair for fashion, style, and adventure may just have me look like that concert-going dude in the year 2030!

McCartney and his pals didn't start out as rock stars. McCartney met John Lennon in 1957 at age fifteen and joined his garage band. It was a spunky little band called the Quarrymen that featured rock music with some jazz, blues, and folk influences. The little group made changes in members (added George Harrison in 1958) and flirted with different names until they officially became the Beatles in 1960. Ringo Starr joined as drummer in 1962, and the rest was history.

For as talented as they were, just forming the band wasn't good enough. In 1961, they were still toiling around Hamburg, Germany, playing clubs and dives, and then they made their first recording. It was there that they serendipitously garnered the attention of Brian Epstein. Epstein became their manager in January of 1962 and is undeniably the key business figure in their development, success, and rapid rise to stardom.

Talent can only take you so far. Too many business professionals, in trying to craft a career, get stuck in the dreary "clubs and dives" of the business world. Had Brian Epstein never entered the lives of the Beatles, who knows what the outcome would have been? I surmise that Barb and I wouldn't have been at Safeco Field in 2013 belting out "Hey Jude" with him and forty thousand of our closest friends. To go from Garage Band to Rock Star, one needs coaching, mentoring, accountability, and guidance. That's where you and your system come in.

My first job out of college was working as a personal lines underwriter for a company called United Pacific Insurance near Seattle. Once I was hired, they wasted no time in setting me up with my first mentor and coach, John Blodnick. John was a great guy. He was a young man who had quickly risen in the ranks and had reached a managerial level. He had already garnered a tremendous amount of respect from those in the office.

He set out a detailed schedule for Brian (another new employee) and me. Every aspect of the job that we would be doing was covered. It included interviews with other veteran underwriters, case study work, skills testing, and other things that, nearly thirty years later, I think have been lost somewhere in my memory banks. To say that he was detail-oriented would be accurate.

The more important thing, however, had little to do with the methodology of teaching us insurance, risk factors, and procedures. The most important thing John provided Brian and me was a mentoring style that was respectful, genuine, and accessible. John had mastered the art and science of mentoring and coaching without even knowing he was doing it. He knew exactly how to help his protégés most rapidly advance in their jobs and careers. Ironically enough for me, I quickly realized that underwriting wasn't for me. The job didn't match my social style or strengths, so after eighteen months I left for the agency side of insurance. John had trained me well, and often training will include the determination of whether you're in the right spot. To this day, I'm grateful to John for his guidance, candor, and support.

Fast forward to 1989 when I joined my first insurance agency. I was placed in a small, rural office setting, given a desk and some manuals (remember 1989—almost zero technology) and a stout pat on the back with a "Go get 'em, son!"

While I eventually did "go get 'em," the stark difference between the onboarding of the two jobs is significant. Even though I stayed longer at the second job, the training I received from John Blodnick was exceptionally better. Now, twenty-five-plus years later, you can't get away with the latter example (regardless of the size of your business) and hope to turn new employees into rock stars. You may find they get stuck in that garage so long that they bolt out the back door.

So how do you go about maximizing the talents of those new employees to help them rise to the top more quickly? If you're one of those garage band members, what can you do to make an impact that will enhance whatever help you're getting?

The first step in this process for you as a leader is to assess the potential growth of your employee. Just because a kid in a garage is playing a guitar, it doesn't mean they are any good at it. Confidence doesn't always equal competence. Assessments aren't usually easy, and if you're basing all of your judgment solely on tools like DISC profiles, Caliper testing, or Myers-Briggs results, you're making a huge mistake. While these tests can be utilized as *one* evaluative tool, way too many organizations place all their eggs in that basket during the hiring process. This greatly devalues the actual skills and ability to learn of the people in question and can often place them in a box that they may never be able to climb out of, and may ultimately hasten their exit to greener pastures.

There was a time when people were hired without being asked to differentiate between their likes and dislikes, how often they think about humankind and its destiny, or if they prefer peanut butter and jelly over ham and cheese. You are undoubtedly skilled enough to ask the right questions to determine the perspicacity and upside of your "garage-bander." Here are my five personal techniques for you to consider using when evaluating where your employees currently are and what talent they have to offer. You won't need a #2 pencil.

1. **Ask them what they want to accomplish in their career.** Sounds too simple, right? It's not. You want people who view their work with you as a career, not a job that leads to their career.

2. **Find out what motivates them.** Is it money, recognition, acceptance, or the actual work? Some may be evasive, or answer the

way they think you want them to. Your future rock stars will likely be honest, yet you will have to be perceptive and continue to ask questions.

3. **Learn about their family and personal life.** You'd be amazed how much you can discern when you understand what makes a person tick. I always ask my new coaching clients to complete a questionnaire that includes queries on their hobbies, favorite foods, and cherished vacation spots. When you understand the whole person, you can better relate to what they need and where they want to go.

4. **Figure out how they best learn.** Are they visual? Auditory? Kinesthetic? Some of the tests I mentioned earlier can help in this area. . .that's a good use for them. Some people learn best by reading, and others, by watching a video. I subscribe to a series hosted by Alan Weiss where his weekly dispatches are provided in print, video, and podcast. How will you most effectively reach your people?

5. **Be flexible.** Nothing ever goes perfectly. Be flexible in your approach, be ready and willing to change, and absolutely keep the lines of honest communication open. It's okay to shift course if needed or desired. Remember that famous quote that has been attributed to Albert Einstein, (yet probably wasn't his): "Insanity is doing the same thing over and over again and hoping for a different result." Be willing to implement change.

It's one thing to inspire yourself. It's quite another to inspire others. The greatest at their craft aren't automatically qualified to lead others to greatness. The world of sports is littered with examples of the world's greatest athletes who bombed as coaches. It takes a lot more than mere ability to masterfully transfer that skill to others.

For a span of about a decade, Tiger Woods was the greatest golfer on the planet. In fact, I believe he may be the greatest single athlete of my generation from a sheer dominance standpoint, and that includes Michael Jordan and Wayne Gretzky. Yet Tiger Woods had coaches. He had coaches who helped him with his swing, his putting, his short game, and the mental side of competing. None of these experts could play the game like him. However, without their influence, he wouldn't have been able to either.

One of the biggest mistakes I see in business is turning rock star sales professionals into mediocre-at-best sales managers. The assumption is that they aspire to coaching and managing others. In my experience, sales professionals who are superior aren't wired to teach and mentor others, just like Larry Bird wasn't adept at coaching professional basketball, although he was a living legend.

If you are tasked with (or just as importantly, tasking someone else with) guiding and growing greatness within your organization, then there are specific attributes and actions to be considered. This chapter is more about Vince Lombardi than Joe Montana. Identifying the right person, giving them the right tools, and then letting them do their *thing* will deliver championship results for your organization. I submit to you my **9 Rules for Cranking Up the Volume on Your Garage Band**. . .

Rule #1: **Assess.** You've hired someone to do a job. At some point during the hiring process (if done correctly), your hiring committee came to the conclusion that this person was right for the role. They probably did that by seeing the potential employee's strengths, skills, and talents in areas that were required for the job.

How do you determine what you have in a new employee? I suppose you can spend an inordinate amount of time going through the reports of all the testing you put him or her through during the hiring process. However, I'm a little "old school" on this. I believe the powers of observation and listening are far more reliable.

This is where patience is important. Do you remember being a new employee? It took a little bit of time in the beginning to find your way and learn the culture of a place. There was heightened anxiety as you learned names, roles, and responsibilities.

Now, as a leader, this is an ideal time for you to simply observe. You had an idea of this person's strengths coming in because you hired them. Find out if he or she is legitimate. Watch how the new employee interacts with others, give some "tests" to measure reactions, and ask lots of questions to probe for responses. This isn't dissimilar to a football coach watching a rookie in training camp. You need to assess what you have.

Rule #2: Focus on strengths, not weaknesses.

The focus of your training now shouldn't be on the things new employees can't do well. Focus on the things they already do well and enhance them.

I work with many clients who have a vision for an employee (new or veteran). The vision is based on what they want that employee to do, not on what the employee is good at doing. If you've got a strong sales professional and you envision them taking their expertise and becoming a rock star sales manager, you're making a mistake. If you've got a solid worker who cranks out widgets like they are going out of style, transitioning them into a managerial position might just lose you both a good worker and a manager.

I've got a client who spent a great deal of time and effort on their best employee, trying to turn them into a potential perpetuation plan. This employee was lights out as a worker, and when approached about ownership, was happy. Who wouldn't be flattered and excited about being asked to "move up" into a management or ownership position? The results, however, weren't as good. The employee simply wasn't wired for managing people, dealing with conflict, and creating sales relationships. These were all strengths of the owner, and he needed someone to take on that role. The burden on the employee was great. He felt he was letting the owner down. He dreaded coming to work. And his regular job suffered. The detachment of going back was painful. My client viewed this employee as entrepreneur material because he was skilled at the methodology of the job. His vision was tainted.

You have people in your organization whom you want to advance who have no skill or perspicacity in higher levels of management. Instead of trying to fit those round pegs into square holes until one or both break, give them a raise in pay (or other reward or incentive) and enhance the skills they are so good at. You will end up with happier employees, better results on the work, and a better organizational culture.

Rule #3: Set real expectations. One of the biggest mistakes that people in position of training or mentoring make is that expectations are never established. There need to be specific (and sometimes measurable) expectations set regarding:

1. Training schedules
2. Communications (internally and externally)
3. Mentoring and coaching assignments
4. What success looks like
5. Consequences of not meeting expectations
6. Results and rewards for exceeding expectations
7. Culture within the organization
8. Industry specific criterion
9. Ongoing professional development
10. Reimbursement of expenses

You may have others that fit your company or organization. Add those in as you see fit. These expectations can't be expected to "reside" in everyone's brain. They need to be written (electronically is fine) and affirmed by signature by all parties so that the expectations are clear.

I have a client who uses a *team agreement*. The executive team has laid out what their expectations are regarding team culture and how everyone interacts professionally and personally. Employees sign off that they have read the team agreement and will abide by the expectations. While this may sound overly formal, it's not. It's a pretty simple yet specific document that lays the ground rules for organizational success through relationships. The very same thing can be accomplished for setting expectations when training new employees.

Rule 4: Train the trainers. One of my clients is a naval installation within the Department of Defense. Russ, a colleague of mine in Rotary, had approached me at a meeting and asked if I did training programs for people who wanted to be mentors. He was a subscriber to my newsletter and read stories about my work as a mentor. As head of training and development for this installation, he was looking for someone to teach a bunch of engineers how to be mentors. It turned out that the Navy as a whole had sent down orders that mentoring was a requirement for all installations. Russ was worried that asking people who had no experience (nor had ever been trained as mentors) was a recipe for disaster. He was very forward thinking. Over the next couple of weeks, we put together a two-day program to help these engineers learn skills in strategy and tactical-based mentoring.

As I've stated before, just because someone is *good* at something doesn't mean they will excel in teaching it to others. Even if they are well-intentioned and want to, not having adequate training in mentoring places a hardship on them and the person being trained.

This doesn't have to be complex. There are a myriad of ways to gain even basic training for those that want to be taught the intricacies of being a good mentor and guide. The key point is that if you are going to make the investment in training new employees to attain rock star status, you need to ensure that those training them are qualified to get them there. Remember that old computer adage of "garbage in, garbage out"? That theory also holds true in training and developing people. You need to make sure what's going in is beneficial to reap the results you want. Training the trainer needs to be a component of that investment.

Rule 5: Commit to access. Everyone must be on the same page for accessibility. This can cause the most problems if left unclear. From a new employee's perspective, they need to have easy access ranging from in-person, to phone, to email, and to text. The times of accessibility need to be made clear and be agreed on. Normally, the trainer (might be you) has other duties that demand time. That's why documenting minimums, like when you will call back after a voice mail (or any correspondence), is critical. When I work with my clients, my minimums are ninety minutes for voice mail and text (business hours) and twenty-four hours for email.

Rule 6: Use technology for good. Often there might be an age difference between those training and those being trained. I believe it's the responsibility of the trainer to comply with what works best for the person being trained.

Use technology in a manner that makes sense for the learners to help them grow faster. In communications, you can use text messaging. In methodology work, use videos. And in studying, make use of tablets, apps, and other mobile devices to get the point across more quickly.

Rule 7: Measure the success. Alan Weiss often uses the query "How would you know it if you tripped over it?" when describing metrics. At some foundational level, you and those you train need to know if they are succeeding. Collaboratively setting metrics at the outset, keeping track of progress, making adjustments as needed, and recognizing and rewarding success. . .these are the best ways to ensure that your garage band pupil is heading towards stardom. And more importantly, that's how they know too!

Rule 8: Praise early and often. It's easy to be lax in this area. I think it's simply human nature to focus on the areas you want improved in others without offering enough praise for achievement. I was guilty of this when I coached basketball. Today, as a coach of adult business professionals, I make it a priority to remember to tell people I am proud of them when they make progress. The feeling of satisfaction is palpable, even when we are on the phone. You like an occasional pat on the back. So will the people who look to you as a guide.

Rule 9: Have fun. Pretty simple. Life is too short to not enjoy what you're doing. If the job in and of itself is tedious, then you might have the wrong person for the job. Things get "out of fun" when there are unclear or unattainable expectations, when there is command and no collaboration, when everyone takes themselves too seriously, and when no measures of success are being created, much less attained. Employees leave jobs not just for financial considerations. In fact, if you read Daniel Pink's book *Drive*, you will see he postulates that salary is one of the lower considerations when choosing to stay with a job. Being able to say you're having fun in what you spend the bulk of your waking hours doing not only has merit, but also may be the ultimate determinant of whether your prized pupil becomes a rock star with you or someone else.

Extra Point: One of my favorite people in the world is a guy named Jerry Parrish. Jerry was head football coach and PE teacher at North Kitsap High School for nearly four decades. Jerry is a colleague (we coached at the same time), a client (in his eighties he still is executive secretary for the coaches association that hires me), and a dear friend. He retired in 2006 from both coaching and teaching. I vividly recall chatting with him over a cup of coffee shortly after his retirement. He told me something I will always remember. He said, with a modest smile, "Dan, I never considered myself having a job. I just never left school, and I loved school!" Wouldn't it be great if we could all say the same thing?

A Captain Jack Extra Point
Simplicity Rules

Simplicity is the answer.

That's why we dogs are so smart. We never overcomplicate things. We don't overthink or get overwhelmed. We just overcome through simplicity. That's where we have it all over you humans.

Take me, for example. I get up every morning excited for the day, because I have no idea what's going to happen. I'm open to what happens in the moment. I know I'm going to be fed, get some exercise, maybe do some writing, bark at squirrels and rabbits, and enjoy a few power naps. Pretty simple.

When things happen that are out of my control, I do the best I can. It's not always perfect, but I don't expect myself to be perfect. I expect to do my best. No matter what happens, I'm content with myself, my effort, and I move on to another power nap. Simple.

A lot of humans try to predict their day, like that would actually help. Some start the morning off complaining before there is anything to complain about. Many are nervous, anxious, or bored. When an event or crisis outside of their control happens, they deal with it too. However, there are a lot of you who then become obsessed with how you did. Look, if you do the best you can at the time, then that's all you can do. Stop making things so complicated because it gets in the way of you being better. If we dogs did that all of the time, we'd be a whimpering mess.

If you want to live a more simple, dog-like life, then simplify your life. You guys try to do too much. Find what you like and do it. Find whom you like and be with them. If you make a mistake, learn and move on. If you try too hard, you're probably going to fail. Cut yourself some slack and be happy. Then go get a power nap. It always works for me.

> *Just saying. . .*
> Captain Jack

The Sustainability System

HOW TO STAY THE LEAD DOG

It was about 1994 around the Christmas holiday season. We went as a family to the local pet store to have a picture taken with Santa. Mindy and Kelli were about six and five years old, respectively, and our first family dog, Blondie, was a rambunctious three-year-old terrier mix. All dogs were required to be leashed in the store, yet with her it was an absolute necessity due to her penchant for being a "runner." The girls (including Barb) were all dressed up in their Christmas best, and I had my best "ugly sweater" on. As we approached to sit with Santa, the photographer suggested we dispense with the leash to improve the picture. Knowing my dog well, I was a little dubious. I also knew this was one of those pictures that needed to look good for eternity, so we did it. I can have a firm grip on my dog when necessary. Santa Claus wasn't as skilled.

As soon as Blondie had hopped on the chubby cherub's lap, she then bounded off in the opposite direction, ready to see the store. The girls squealed with glee, thinking this was so much fun. Barb (not so amused), exclaimed in a stern voice, "Go get the dog." Easier said than done. While I was much younger and spryer twenty years ago, I was no match for Blondie. She never had to run at full speed. She knew exactly how fast I could run while maneuvering around people, dogs, and supplies. She was able to stay just one step ahead of me, in the lead. The chase probably only lasted four to five minutes, although it seemed much longer. Finally, she darted into the food section (olfactory senses in full canine mode). I was able to corner and corral her. As we walked back to Santa, there were plenty of people smiling and laughing, with my daughters leading the applause. I still grin when looking at that picture today. The expression on Blondie's face affirms that she knew what she was doing all along.

Blondie "played me" during my pursuit. She never had to resort to an all-out sprint. She was able to always stay just a step out of arms reach for as long as she wanted to. She stayed the lead dog.

Much too often, we humans dart out to a big lead by "sprinting" to our destination. We exert so much energy that we can't maintain it and eventually lose momentum and the lead. Ultimately, this can result in giving up too soon and a loss of confidence.

An example would be coming up with a great new initiative or idea and then putting all your effort and time into it. It gets off to a quick start, and there is a lot of expectation and hope. Suddenly, you hit a "speed bump," and momentum is lost and doubt creeps in. Before you know it, the initiative or idea is shelved before it ever had a chance to succeed.

Initiatives and ideas, like so many other things, need to be nourished and allowed to endure. Staying "in the lead" without "sprinting" and overwhelming yourself is most often the best tack to take. It allows for sudden and unforeseen changes, shifts in momentum, and the ability to be resilient. Expending too much energy too fast can be bad, even in what you might consider a "sprint" situation. Staying in the lead is critical to staying strong through to the finish line. As a leader, you may just be the lead dog on a project, mandate, or initiative. Whether it's your own company or one you have responsibility for, its success is determined by your ability to stay in front and keep momentum going regardless of circumstances. This chapter is about doing just that.

Big Mo

Why Momentum Matters

I admit it. I was wrong. Well. . .sort of.

Many of you who have read my work over the years might recall that I've written before about "finishing strong" and how success is not about how you start, but how you finish. I didn't make this concept up, of course. Any of you who have followed business, sports, or cooking know this idea.

Extra Point: If you're wondering why I mention cooking, you might be surprised about what I mean. Certainly finishing cooking meat, fish, or any other main dish is not only critical to its success, but also to ensuring you're not poisoning your guest! But I encourage you to think about the importance of "plating." This is truly "finishing" a dish in a fine restaurant. All chefs will tell you that you eat with your eyes first. This finish is as important as any other factor outside of the actual taste. Now back to our regularly scheduled programming. . .

While the concept of running hard through the finish line is a sound business analogy (you know, the whole "winning by a nose" thing), I think there is a bigger and better concept to consider. This is the concept that there is actually no finish line at all.

Finish lines imply the end of the race. Usain Bolt is considered the fastest person in the world because he can almost fly over a one-hundred-meter track. An Olympic Games one-hundred-meter race has a tangible conclusion, along with winners and losers. On the other hand, your business, your career, and your life don't. And yes, I acknowledge we are not immortal and will eventually die. That's a finish line of a different sort, so let's focus our attention on the rest of the races!

We have many "starts and stops" in our lives. They can occur regularly within the course of even one day! The truth is that if we just stop after running hard through one finish line, then we may just miss an all-important "next race." In essence, we lose momentum.

A couple of years ago, I received a frantic call from an insurance agents association in Montana. It turned out that one of their instructors for a new professional designation course took ill and had to cancel on them. This left the association with a full class of forty people and nobody to teach. They were given my name as the next nearest qualified instructor. Fortunately, there was no conflict and I was able to fly to Billings the following week and teach the workshop. The conclusion of the class might have denoted the "finish line." I'm glad I didn't stop "running."

Before I left, I asked about other opportunities for the association to have me come speak. As it turned out, my contact was very interested and in charge of conferences and events. Through additional conversations, this "race" has been extended to speaking at two conferences over successive years and teaching another continuing education workshop. From a business standpoint, the revenue and contacts far exceeded that initial project. Had I simply packed up my bags after that first "race," I would have missed a tremendous opportunity to grow my business and brand.

Now it's your turn. What opportunities have you missed because you stopped running? Have you given up because an answer was "no"? Did you not consider the possibilities of extending projects or relationships because they were assumed to be completed? Did you just forget to follow up on a promise? My guess is that the answers to these questions are "yes." I am as guilty as anyone, and now I intentionally commit to sustaining the race as long as possible. All of these questions, if answered affirmatively, eventually lead to loss of "Big Mo."

A "race" is a mindset. "Finish lines" are simply a metaphor indicating that the work is done, that it's over. This might be a client engagement or an event. It also applies to your ongoing professional development. I've encountered many people who thought they "knew it all." There was no need of further learning or of challenging themselves. Unfortunately, this thinking can also pervade our personal lives, thus thwarting our change and growth as individuals.

One important note to remember: if there is no finish line, there are no losers. We may try and fail constantly, and this is expected. Those who don't have many failures are usually those who are afraid of trying. We run many races, and some have natural conclusions, yet they lead right to the starting blocks of other important contests. Competition isn't reserved for athletes. Certainly you have competition in business, yet too many people don't think of it in the correct way. Competition is often viewed as one combatant against another, dueling it out until there is a winner and loser. Real competition is internal. It's about striving to do your best in that race, that moment, that day. When you compete internally, you won't lose as long as you did the best you could. All too often, I hear from people I coach that they aren't satisfied with their best effort. This is an insidious mental cramp that will keep you from being able to run your races well. You can only do your best with what you have. When that's not good enough for one race, you simply move the next one.

There is no finish line. Your career and life are a series of races run not only simultaneously, but also concurrently. This means you have to be an "athlete." That requires agility, nimbleness, concentration, desire, focus, persistence, strength, flexibility, and power.

As you read this chapter, consider that the "no finish line" concept requires that you keep momentum going. Runners must keep their legs and arms pumping in order to keep inertia from setting in. With no finish line, there is no stopping. Momentum continues on at a steady pace. That's what you want in your business and career.

Setting & Managing Organizational Expectations

Expectations that are communicated to everyone and are met lead directly to your best performance and outcomes. That's not a shocking statement or novel concept. Unfortunately, the implementation of this concept is often modest at best and shoddy at worst. The problem is that expectations lack clarity in many organizations. They may be bandied about on mission statement posters and websites, yet the vision and motives behind the verbiage fall short in strategy, communication, discipline and monitoring. Let's discuss each.

Strategy: When was the last time you were in charge of setting expectations but never strategized over what they were, why you wanted them, and how to implement them? For me, it came during my tenure as a school board president. As leaders of a $60 million "business," we had annual goals set. The problem was that they were often flimsy because they lacked clarity, metrics, and communication. One of my colleagues had the "bright idea" that we should allocate some of our time to strategic planning, and she was right. While we may have had good reasons the previous two years for not doing this (we were dealing with the crisis of closing a school), the time had come to stop skipping this vital first step.

Strategic planning requires you as a leader to create a vision for long-term sustainability of culture and operations. This means sophisticated and candid discussions on recruiting, hiring practices, onboarding, training, and other factors that figure into your specific company. What is your vision? What do you want the company to look like in three years? In five years? You start with building a vision because without a destination, you will easily get distracted and lost.

Strategic planning should involve the key members of your organization. For Fortune 500 companies, this is the smallest of subsets in a large organization. For a small family-owned business, it might be everyone at the table! Regardless, you're making a big mistake by thinking that sustaining behaviors and activities just happens on its own. You need to identify exposures and perils to sustainability, plan for the possibility of bad things happening, put contingency plans in place, and then monitor your progress.

Communications: Communications is the lifeblood of significant strategic initiatives. I can't count the number of clients I talked to at the outset of our work together who had laid good foundations for success yet missed telling their employees about it!

I once worked on a "crisis improv" project with a client. I would give the CEO and his leadership team a crisis scenario that they weren't expecting, and we would then "play it out." Shortly into the exercise, I asked my client if he had a crisis communication plan. He proudly puffed out his chest and asserted, "Yes, we do!" His chest shrunk when I asked, "Good. What does it say to do?" It was clear he didn't know. To add fuel to the fire, the director of technology piped up and said, "While we may have a plan, it's no good." I asked why he said that. He answered, "Too often, my subordinates come to me asking about a crisis situation and what to do next, and I didn't even know about it. The chain of information is flawed. I should know before them." And he was right.

This client had a plan but did an awful job of communicating it to his leadership team and employees. This is like having a fine bottle of wine with no opening to pour from.

Part of the strategic work is carefully crafting a plan to disseminate information (in proper order) to the entire organization. I'm not saying to merely post your mission and values statement outside the restroom door. I mean assuring that all employees know what your vision and culture are, what is expected of them in terms of behaviors and activities, what they can expect for professional growth, and what to do in a crisis (this will be covered in the subsequent chapters).

Discipline: Nobody likes to talk about discipline. The reality is that you can't be a business owner or leader and never have to deal with conflict and behavioral issues. In fact, the majority of my work as a consultant and coach was initiated because of unwanted behavior and clients not knowing how to deal with it effectively.

This subsection isn't designed to give you answers to every possible disciplinary scenario. That would be a book all to itself. What you will find is a template to use for virtually every possible situation from both a preventative and contingent viewpoint.

1. Define what "bad" behavior is. I would make this as easy as possible. When I coached high school basketball, I had only one rule for a group of twenty-five teenage girls: don't let your teammates down. These seemingly simple five words carry a lot of flexibility and amazing clarity at the same time. Whatever is deemed undesirable in your culture—lying, stealing, bullying, social media surfing, and harassment—needs to be identified. Example: While poor behavior seems conspicuous, it happens in offices and operations across the world every day. There are reams of research indicating that employees are "stealing" time and resources by surfing the Internet daily while they are supposed to be working. A 2010 survey showed that the insurance industry was the "leader in the clubhouse," averaging two and a half hours per employee per day of being distracted online by social media, porn, and seeking new jobs.[8] Most employees don't think twice about the ramifications of lost time, productivity, and opportunity associated with this, not to mention the issue of literally taking money for no work.

2. Once you've, as an organization, defined bad behavior, now you have to share your definition. This shouldn't be doled out as a reproduction of the Ten Commandments being presented to Moses on Mount Sinai. Instead, there should be a clear statement on the most egregious behaviors and how those will be dealt with—hand slap to suspension to termination.

    Give people the credit they deserve as being adults, yet as former U. S. president Ronald Reagan once said about the Soviet Union, "Trust, but verify." Ironically, Mr. Reagan borrowed this saying from a Russian proverb. Go figure.

3. Be consistent. The one thing that will alienate your employees

---

8 American Management Association, "New Survey Shows Time's a Wastin'—Workers Goof Off More Than Two Hours a Day," AMA website, August 5, 2010, http://www.amanet.org/training/articles/New-Survey-Shows-Times-a-Wastin-and-mdash;Workers-Goof-Off-more-than-Two-Hours-a-Day.aspx. Referencing a survey done by America Online and Salary.com.

the quickest is lack of consistency in discipline. Just because a guy is your best sales person doesn't mean he gets a free pass on boorish or unethical behavior. While this concept might seem as obvious as a dog wagging its tail when he's happy, it gets violated often. You have undoubtedly worked in situations where the "stars" (leadership included) are afforded different rules than everyone else.

4. Privacy and protection. Social media has made it much more difficult to keep things discreet. If discipline is needed, then make sure all parties know that it's an "in-house" event. What do I mean by protection? Document everything in writing. Get appropriate signatures on any documents to confirm understanding. Make sure you have witnesses to corroborate discussions and decisions.

Taking disciplinary steps is never easy, but it is necessary for the good of the entire organization. Leaders who avoid dealing with issues due to disliking conflict, fear of consequences, or any other reason risk eroding the culture and killing any momentum that has been established.

Monitoring. Later in this chapter, we will discuss *gravitational pull*. For now, we can probably agree that it's human nature to allow some slippage in even the best ideas and concepts. Someone has to be at the switch and have authority to reverse that slippage. Observation and quick fixes are stalwart qualities for an Unleashed leader. You might delegate parts of this, but don't fool yourself. You are ultimately responsible for assuring that the work you have done to build momentum continues. Otherwise, all your time, effort, and investment will have been wasted.

Cultivating Leaders Who Police Themselves

One of the constants I hear from business owners and executives I work with is the desire for their teams to be able to "police" themselves. At a basic level, to create a group of people who can collaborate to deal with inevitable issues is nirvana for the business leader. If one of your jobs as the head honcho is playing referee to all the drama and conflict in your company, then you will find very little time to do the things that you most like to do and are the most skilled at doing!

This book started by discussing the concept of "playing for each other." Being able to collectively find solutions to challenges and leaving egos and agendas at the door is a hard thing to cultivate. We discussed how to get your team to play for each other. Once that has been accomplished, this second part is easier.

Three elements are needed to ensure that this very important piece of your puzzle is going to work. These three elements are trust, authority, and what I term "the consultant."

Trust. This comes from you, not necessarily them. When I was coaching basketball, there were always situations where I needed to completely trust my assistant coaches. It's easy for basketball coaches (or any sports coach) to get very astigmatic and obstinate in their ways of doing things. I realized this in myself and had to force myself to trust my very capable assistant coaches to follow through with issues around play calling, discipline, and player substitutions. While I always had the final say (stay tuned for *consultant*), I needed to show them that I had faith in their discernment and expertise, and also show the players I was willing to walk the talk when preaching trust.

Running a business isn't much different, especially if you are the founder. You can become unbending when it comes to fully trusting someone else with your "baby." The reality is that if you are assembling a group of employees to carry out your vision, which may ultimately be your legacy, then trusting in good people (unless they are shown otherwise with empirical data) will only help you reach your goals.

Final thought on trust: This is easier said than done. I guarantee you Captain Jack and his fellow canines trust their masters until given reason not to. They have unconditional trust, and it serves them well. They can go off and run through gates all over the place if they have no concerns that there will be water for them to drink and a comfy bed when they return. You have to get to a point where you internally believe in your team so your team can also believe in you.

Authority. One of the unkindest cuts of all is to come up with solutions to problems and have little to no authority to implement them. Granting authority is part and parcel of trust, yet it has other components too. Trust without authority is akin to letting someone close down the store at the end of the evening but not giving him or her the password for setting the alarm.

If you're at a point where you want your team to solve problems, you will also need to grant authority to at least one member of that team to dispense discipline, make agreements, and move forward on initiatives or projects.

Trust can be hard to fully embrace until time has passed. Authority can be much easier. In fact, I've encountered cases where authority is all too freely given out when it's not deserved! As an Unleashed leader, you want to open gates of opportunity to your subordinates and direct reports, and to your employees and staff. Trust and authority must be equally present. Here's why:

Trust without full authority equals a control freak. You think your people are great, but you can't relinquish anything and become buried in work and refereeing others. **Authority without trust** is like giving the keys to the henhouse to the wolf. Allowing authority when it hasn't been fully earned borders on apathy and complacency. . .or ignorance. The equality of trust and authority means a healthy balance in the relationship and culture.

The Consultant. That's you! There probably will always be a need for your sage wisdom and guidance. Your team must also trust that they can ask you for advice and guidance without you jumping in and meddling, or taking any of their authority away. Part of the job of Unleashed leaders is to mentor those dogs running behind them. By making yourself available to do this, you will be cultivating leadership skills and confidence.

Here's an important tactic for your consideration: Always make them come to you with a solution that you can comment and offer opinions on. If they get in the habit of merely bringing the problem for you to solve, then they aren't learning anything. In my mentoring relationship with Alan Weiss, I've worked hard to always approach him with a problem-solution inquiry. That way, I'm simply checking my work. It's led to more sophisticated discussions and an increased level of confidence in my decision-making. The same will happen for your team.

Gravitational Pull
How to Avoid a Freefall Into Monotony and Misery

We are all familiar with the work of Sir Isaac Newton on the theory of gravity. That small red apple that presumably bounced of Sir Isaac's noggin showed that the magnetic pull from the earth would force objects down to the ground. That is the simple version; I was never much of a physics student. Much like Sir Isaac's theory, my term *gravitational pull* involves the return to "earth" of your own poor habits, activities, and behaviors. I define *gravitational pull* this way:

> *Gravitational pull* is the human desire to return to the default position of comfort and complacency. It occurs at points along the journey from the current state to the desired state. It's the hidden and calamitous situation that, if gone unchecked, will ensure that no growth occurs and decline becomes inevitable.

I'm fascinated by the mechanics of being a good NFL quarterback. These guys all grew up as gifted athletes, rose in prominence through the elite ranks in high school and college, and ended up in the National Football League. Even the backups were once star quarterbacks at the college level.

Tim Tebow was a standout quarterback at the University of Florida. He was a two-time All-American, a two-time National Champion, and the 2007 Heisman Trophy winner. He accomplished these feats by being an incredible athlete. Unfortunately, he had mediocre "mechanics" for the NFL. His poor mechanics led him to be inaccurate in his passing. The pro league relies more on this skill than the ability run, which was one of Tebow's strengths.

When Tebow entered the NFL, many coaches started working with him to change his mechanics. Tebow is a smart guy and a great athlete and worked hard in practice to improve. The problem always came in the game. It's one thing to be able to calmly practice your new mechanics when it really doesn't matter. It's quite another when you're in live action and being chased around by three-hundred-pound defensive ends! Tebow would revert to his "default" mechanics under pressure, which left him too inaccurate for the pro game. As successful as he had been in college, he has struggled to take that next step.

The same can be said for us in the business world. As we climb the tiers on our careers, what may have made us successful once might actually be holding us back from future "glory." We may be smart and acknowledge our shortcomings, define our desired state of betterment, and even implement the changes necessary. But along the way, we have our own defensive ends chasing us, and we revert to our old ways. Just like Newton's apple is forced to the ground, our comfortable ways are pulling us back like a magnet.

We have many terms for this phenomenon, "human nature" being the most prominent. But that's a cop out. In order to grow both professionally and personally, we need to overcome our own *gravitational pull*. In order to be effective leaders, we must be able to identify it in others and help them to overcome. Otherwise, the individual *gravitational pulls* will ultimately drag down the company.

The concept is pretty easy. The identification and solutions tend to be a little more arduous. Let's start by identifying the hurdles that are the proximate causes of failing to finish the race:

1. **Time.** This may be easily the biggest culprit. The pressure of time is as real to us in the business world as that three-hundred-pound defensive end is to NFL quarterbacks! When time becomes a factor, we revert to what is easy. At first, we know we shouldn't break our newfound mechanics, yet it will only be this one time, right? Wrong. It's a slippery slope.

Let's consider an example. I am a decent Spanish speaker; however, because of my family roots, I want to be more than just decent. I want to be excellent. I know how to accomplish this too. I purchased Rosetta Stone and other Spanish speaking aids to help me accelerate my learning. I made a time commitment of a minimum of fifteen minutes a day. For the first month, I was golden. Then all of a sudden, things got a little busier. I added new clients. Some projects became time sensitive. My mother's health was deteriorating. My non-work commitments were becoming more pressing. A perfect storm, right? The consequence was that I would take days off from practicing my Spanish. Days off suddenly turned into weeks off. You see the pattern developing. . .months came next. My Spanish had been forced down by *gravitational pull*. As I write this, I've restarted the process and am using my good advice on myself!

Time will always be an enemy. Know this upfront and prepare for it. I was recently given outstanding advice from Alan Weiss. Alan said to add 20 percent to everything you commit time or finances to. In this case, allocate 20 percent more time to your planning because the reality is you will need it. When you need to "create" time for change, make sure you are dropping something else to ensure there is room, and then add 20 percent.

2. **Non-Priority.** Sometimes we lie to ourselves and state we have a priority when we don't. We tell ourselves this change should be a priority, so we say it is. Being honest with yourself about your priorities will keep you from wasting time and ensure that your real priorities get done.

Example: You are forced into going to the gym because you made a New Year's resolution to lose weight. You think it's the right thing to do and have finally committed. The problem with weight loss resolutions is that, more often than not, the person making the resolution really doesn't have the burning desire to change. That makes *gravitational pull* easy.

3. **Distraction.** Distraction is different than time because instead of time becoming a challenge, something else is. It might be a focus on a different priority. You may have been tasked to complete another project. Regardless of the reason for the distraction, understanding that new diversions and interruptions are a part of life when going into a project will help you mitigate the "pull."

4. **Other People.** One of the common distractions that needs its own spot on this list is people. It's easy to be dissuaded from your task by others who will tell you that you're wasting your time. They might grouse that the change isn't necessary, you won't be better off, or a myriad of other negative feedback. Some of it might even be well-intentioned and come from family. Others might come from coworkers or peers. The problem is that in the midst of all the other challenges, the hurdle of "other people" can push you down with rapidity. Understand from the start that all good motives have their naysayers. Be prepared to ignore them.

5. **Failures.** Often new initiatives are met with initial failures. Too many of these can lead to discouragement, and later, to apathy. Being prepared to deal with failure, especially in the beginning, is paramount to ensuring that the trend is always moving upward.

The very best way to counter the effects of *gravitational pull* is to acknowledge the existence of it and what the hurdles are. You're off to a good start just by reading this past section. Let's use a visual to provide you with a "plug and play" example:

181

Success

Figure 9.1

Plan means to expect hurdles to come. It's the most obvious starting spot because so many of us just ignore this basic reasoning.

Prepare means to put contingency plans in place to mitigate the hurdles and propel you back on track.

Grind means simply to *grind* through the muck and mud and be resilient. Golfers often talk about "grinding" through the tough holes in a round. What it means for you is persevering.

Let's say you are implementing a change in your sales process. You introduce new language skills, an improved tracking system, and team role-plays to practice. Everyone is giddily on board at the beginning.

Plan: You have to plan for hurdles. You can probably name a number yourself including, initial failures, grumbling and whining from within, and loss of motivation and priority.

Prepare: Communicate with everyone what the potential hazards are. Discuss initial failures and how they might affect morale. Challenge people to stay vigilant and positive. Give them an avenue to seek a place to vent or gain guidance and support. That avenue might even be to come talk to you!

Grind: This is where you will find out if you (and your team) are mentally tough. If overcoming *gravitational pull* is truly a priority and you believe it is worth your investment of time and money, then battling through the hurdles is necessary. This is where Unleashed leadership is at its best. It's where you can inspire, communicate, and lead by example. In the end, the "grinding" part will be the glue that keeps you together in your project. The more times you must persevere through hurdles, the more reason you will have to continue. It's easier to quit after one failure than it is after enduring ten failures.

Gravitational pull is a stark reality. People with grit, mental toughness, and a strong self-discipline defeat it. We all struggle with this. I am able to write about it because I still fight it every day. Self-doubts and loss of motivation happen to all of us. Those who remain positive and know that the rewards of the journey will be great are able to overcome it. As the leader, you will be the fulcrum. Make sure that you've got the resiliency and fortitude to conquer *gravitational pull* yourself so you can help others do the same.

A Captain Jack Extra Point
Groundwork

I'm low to the ground. Really low compared to humans. My drop from what Dan calls "gravitational pull" isn't very far. And unlike him, I'm all for it.

You see, I use the weight of gravitational pull to drop down and relax, to sleep, and to pull things out places to chew on. The other day, I dropped down on the ground and rolled my shoulder into a bug. Good times.

We dogs have no problem being "pulled" to the ground, but we have a very different reason. It's where our strength lies. We are good at eating, sleeping, digging, finding, and generally relaxing in the sun. We understand what we are good at it and constantly do it. Humans sometimes either don't know what they are good at (so how can they do it?), or if they do know, they choose to waste time doing things that aren't their strong points. We dogs do our best work on the ground, so we think gravitational pull in reverse. You hu-

mans should figure out what you do well and then focus your attention on it.

Bottom line: Dogs don't waste time doing things we aren't good at. There are too many opportunities out there for us. You should be more like a dog. . . except in reverse. Stay off the ground and reach for the skies.

Just saying. . .
Captain Jack

Prevention is Cheaper

AVOIDING CALAMITY. . .

We live in a residential neighborhood, yet the rear of our house backs up to a greenbelt. While we often see the "usual suspects" like raccoons, squirrels, and rabbits, I've also seen the occasional bear and coyote out and about, looking for food. Any time there is an open gate, access to freedom and adventure awaits. So does danger. This danger of your own allegorical "bears and coyotes" will keep many of you from seeking what lies beyond the gate, and often, up at night fretting.

I'm not sure that Captain Jack (or any dog for that matter) thinks a lot about bears and coyotes when making a decision to bolt through an open gate. That being said, it's ill-advised for you to not at least consider what the challenges are so that you can determine your prevention techniques. Preventing the "bad stuff" from happening is always less expensive than cleaning up the mess. Unlike dogs, we can at least take a moment to perform some due diligence and we should. We just don't need to take too long. Smart people make fast decisions. Determining your own course of action and through which gate it makes most sense to traverse is prudent. Preventing injury and damage is even smarter.

This chapter will help you to quickly identify your own "bears and coyotes" so you can determine your own risk appetite and tolerance.

What Flies Under the Radar Can Kill Your Business

Disaster planning is an executive function. Never forget that. It might be the most important concept you will take away from this chapter. I've met too many CEOs and small business owners who want to delegate disaster planning to others. While the implementation of strategy can and should be delegated, the vision, decisions, and power of the strategy can't be. As a leader, it's yours. As former U. S. president Harry S. Truman once quipped, "The buck stops here."

I once received a video through text from a friend who was vacationing in Kiawah Island in South Carolina. The video was of a hole on the magnificent golf course, which has been host to many pro golf events. The video slowly panned from the tee box and swept over the outline of the hole. I noticed the beautiful lush fairway, the trees guarding the dogleg-right fairway, and the narrowness of the shot that would be required. My focus was solely on the hole and how I might play it. I thought he sent it to me because he knew what a golf enthusiast I am. I was wrong.

My first couple views were from my phone. When I finally watched it from my desktop computer, something new appeared. An alligator. That's right, an alligator coming out of the water to the left of the hole. The gator just slowly and stealthily sauntered through the fairway to the woods on the other side of the hole. My friend was so fascinated by the development of a large gator on the course that he recorded it and shared it with me.

Here's the lesson: I was so focused on what I cared about (the beauty and strategy of the golf hole) that I was oblivious to the peril that was right in front of me. Granted, I wasn't there in person, but the metaphor still works. As a leader of a business, do you ever find yourself so wrapped up in the work that you are oblivious to the perils that walk directly in your path, ready to take a bite out of you?

Fires and floods are common perils that business leaders might mention when thinking of calamity. And why not? Fires and floods make the news in a big way and have catastrophic consequences. However, the likelihood of them happening to your business are remote compared to others that don't get the attention they deserve.

This isn't meant to be an all-encompassing book, or even chapter, on risk management. It's meant to open your eyes to the fact that you're responsible for the well-being of your employees, the continuation of your business, and the affect you have on your clients and community. That means you have to be ready and prepared.

Here's a quick and easy primer for you to use as a leader to help you stay focused on what might saunter out of the lake:

1. **Identify your hazards and perils.** The term *exposures* seems to imply "bad" things, like being "exposed" to second-hand smoke. The truth is that exposures are neither good nor bad. They just are. Exposures in business are buildings, computer systems, parking lots, products, and even people. A quick example would be that your car is "exposed" to a myriad of dangers just because it leaves your garage. That doesn't mean you should avoid driving it. *Perils* are the things that cause damage to property and people—fire, windstorms/hurricanes/tornadoes, cyber attacks, losses of power, auto accidents, slips and falls, and third party liability lawsuits. *Hazards* are those things that cause these perils—frayed and improper wiring, poor housekeeping, inadequate firewalls and protection, poor or inadequate employee training, wet floors, weather, and lack of security. The first and most important step of executive planning is to identify the hazards and perils endemic and specific to your business and industry.

Exposure	Hazard	Peril
• Building • Employee • Technology	• Bad wiring • Bad safety • Poor protection	• Fire • Injury • Data Breach

Figure 10.1

2. **Analyze the data.** Now that you've identified these hazards and perils, what do you do? You need to step back and assess what your data really means.

How likely are some of these perils? While you may live in earthquake country like I do, the reality is that, as bad as one might be, the regularity of it and my ability to control it is minimal. On the other hand, if I live in Florida or South Carolina, I know the hurricanes are coming and need to be more prepared to mitigate them.

What are the frequency and severity risks? Slips and falls in a restaurant or a nursing home are *frequency* issues. So are glass claims for auto fleets. *Severity* risks are less frequent, but more catastrophic—errors and omissions lawsuits, reputation damage, the aforementioned earthquakes and fires, and the death or disability of a worker.

In the example below, you have a situation where the executive or business owner analyzes a worker injury *peril.* In this example, the frequency is moderate (manufacturing). Low frequency might be an office exposure, while high would be construction. The *damage* is listed as high because not only do you face the fallout of that injured worker, but you also lose the productivity and need to find someone to get that work done, which puts stress on the rest of the team, and you might have significantly increased workers' compensation costs.

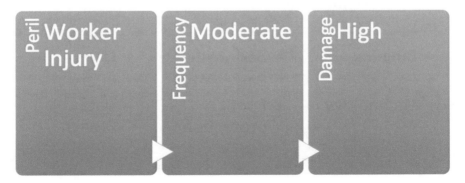

Figure 10.2

3. Mitigate what can't be controlled. You can't control the weather, so if you own a ski resort and you get a winter with very little snow, you'd better have a contingency plan.

Once you've identified and analyzed, it's time to move on to using the tools and resources you do control to reduce the damage and get back to work quickly.

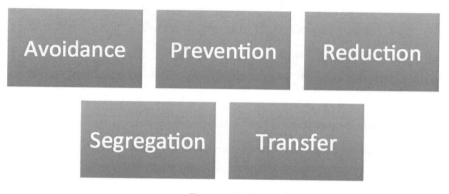

Figure 10.3

Avoidance: Avoidance is totally eliminating an activity or exposure, which eliminates the chance of loss. The reality is that the strategic concept of avoidance is almost always impossible to implement! Usually the product or service that causes the concern is exactly what you do. However, there may be a situation where you come up with a grand idea to increase revenue and are considering implementing it. However, you later find that the consequences might be more harmful than the results are potentially profitable, so you choose not to move forward. For example, I had a client who was considering adding the installation of doors and windows to their lumber sales operations. While they could do it well and make more money, the insurance and risk implications due to the increased likelihood of a claim caused by the unwanted growth of mold or other construction defects didn't make the risk worthwhile.

Prevention: Prevention's goal is to reduce the frequency of types of losses that cannot be eliminated. Loss prevention does not reduce severity; it reduces *frequency*. For example, if you own a restaurant, you can't avoid the threat of slips and falls because that would mean no customers. However, you can improve the traction on the flooring, create wider paths, reduce the number of flooring transfers (e.g., carpet to vinyl), and add more signage around changes in height and stairs. These changes will reduce the frequency of the peril of injured customers, thus avoiding potential liability and loss of reputation.

Reduction: The goal here is to *reduce the severity* or financial impact from losses that are not prevented. If you own a building in hurricane country, you might install additional support and fortify your structure before the big winds hit. If you're in a flood zone, you may have sand bags ready to go. The installation of sprinklers in a building will reduce the severity of a fire.

Segregation/Separation/Duplication: *Segregation* is an isolation of an exposure from other exposures, perils, or hazards. For example, you might segregate or isolate a paint booth or server room from the rest of the building to avoid having another section of the business affect it negatively (or vice versa).

Separation is the spread of exposures or activities over several locations. If you own a large fleet of vehicles and have multiple locations, you might *spread* the risk of damage to your vehicles by having them parked in various locations. One accident (hail, fire) won't affect them all.

Duplication is the use of backups for critical systems or operations. This is backing up your technology and data off-site (e.g., the cloud) to be able to get it back if you lose it on-site.

Transfer: This method is to reduce risk to the organization by transferring some or all of the risk to another party. This can be done contractually (e.g., a lease or hold harmless agreement) or through insurance (see the next section).

4. **Finance your risk.** This is insurance and contracts. I'm not going to bore you with insurance in this book, or even in this section. Well, maybe not *too* much. Here's the deal, as much as you may despise dealing with insurance, you have an obligation to transfer the catastrophic risk you can't afford to pay for out of your own pocket to someone who can. This entails hiring someone who has your best interests at heart, and who has the per-

spicacity to provide protection with the best possible investment by placing it with the right insurers.

5. **Administrate the plan.** This is the hardest part. It requires your support—in both word and deed. The entire team needs to know that you are a leader who demands adherence to the implementation of work that will reduce injuries, enhance business continuation, and ameliorate communication issues in times of distress.

Here is a visual of the key components:

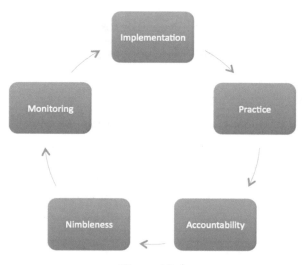

Figure 10.4

Implementation: This doesn't mean you (depending on the size of your company). This means delegating implementations to others. You created the vision and the strategy. Leadership is about engaging and influencing others. Implementations might include:

- Starting a safety committee in charge of employee training (reduce worker injuries)
- Installing ergonomic desks and stations (reduce injuries like carpal tunnel and thoracic outlet syndrome)
- Installing sprinkler system (mitigating fire loss)
- Purchasing and installing automated electronic defibrillators

(save someone's life)

- Add redundancies around technology and communications (mitigate the unavailability of main sources)
- Add a security camera to the front desk and hallways (prevent or reduce external and/or internal violence)
- Create an insurance purchasing process (better ensure protection)
- Add handicapped access to bathrooms (e.g., adherence to the Americans with Disabilities Act and reduction in injuries)
- Install Wi-Fi protections and agreements (reduce liability and potential computer chaos)
- Permanently mount shelving units (avoid them falling on someone in an earthquake)

Practice: We will discuss the practice portion more in the next chapter. Suffice it to say that if you don't know how to do something (or what to do) *before* the crisis, you won't be able to adequately deal with it *during* the crisis. As the leader, you might not even be there, so someone else would be in charge. Imagine the stress and anxiety that is exacerbated by not having a plan and having practiced it!

I call this the "fire extinguisher theory." You undoubtedly have a multitude of fire extinguishers in your place of business (and hopefully, at home). How many of your employees and staff have ever actually pulled the pin and engaged a fire extinguisher? When I ask this question of my clients, they usually chuckle and say "probably very few." Now it may not be your employee's job to put out fires, but extinguishers are there for a purpose. You might as well train everyone on their proper usage.

How about first aid and CPR? How many of your employees are trained? I suggest that they all should be. Not only will this potentially be needed at work, the likelihood that a loved one will need this is pretty high. I once had to give the Heimlich maneuver to my mother when she was choking, and it saved her life. Although I'd never actually used it on a human before, the fact that I'd practiced the maneuver countless times over twenty years made it second nature. You want that from your employees, and it's your job to get them ready and prepared.

Accountability: Remember earlier in the chapter when I quoted President Harry S. Truman? The buck stops with you, and you must not only hold others accountable, you must be accountable as well. This is a tricky thing. With accountability comes additional responsibilities, time commitments, increased knowledge, and increased anxiety and stress.

Let's keep this simple because, in fact, it is. If being ready and prepared for a crisis or disaster is a priority for you, then someone has to be accountable for the plan's implementation and success. It starts with you and goes through the organization. You must give authority to everyone to do the right thing, to make fixes as they are needed, to offer suggestions for improvement, and to tell you when things are going right. In the end, accountability is a culture thing. . .it's the mindset of your company, and it begins with you.

This section isn't meant to give you all the answers but enough to propel you in the right direction. You may need additional training, help from experts, or other tools and resources available in a variety of places. The key is that you are the model for accountability.

I will now jump off my soapbox. . .for the moment.

Nimbleness: Speedboats are more nimble than ocean liners. They can maneuver and take quick actions. They can shift direction with little warning or exertion. The same is true in business. Small businesses are more nimble than their gargantuan brethren. Decisions don't demand endless committee meetings. Accountability is clearer. Authority is more easily granted, as is autonomy.

When it comes to creating a successful strategic crisis plan, nimbleness is also important. The world doesn't stand still. It's much more fluid now due to technology than at any other time in history. That trend will only continue. As you administer your plan, be ready to add, delete, revise, and rethink regularly. I recommend a quarterly review of what you have to ensure that nothing new in the organization needs to be considered. Most times, the current crisis plan will remain unchanged. However, the consequence of not doing regular reviews is that it doesn't take much for your program too quickly become obsolete. And that is usually when the next crisis hits!

Monitoring: This is your *rinse and repeat*. Be observant. I always encourage my clients to simply walk around and observe, talk to people and ask questions, and make sure the implementations they desire haven't fallen into the clutches of *gravitational pull*.

Monitoring sounds easy, but it requires discipline. Discipline from you and from your team. The consequences of not monitoring are wasted time, energy, and money, as well as the likelihood that you will suffer a calamity that you may have otherwise avoided. The results of being diligent in this area are saved time, saved money, and reduced frustration and anxiety. It means that your business continuation is substantially more likely in the event of an uncontrollable crisis. It means that you are assuring your employees and your clients of continued service.

I know this section isn't as sexy as other leadership topics, which fits into my point. Too many CEOs and presidents look at strategic crisis and disaster planning as a nuisance and something to be delegated. If you look at it as an opportunity to create sustainability and to thrive during a challenge, then you can leave an indelible positive mark on your company and those you have responsibility over. It's truly about business building.

It Will Never Happen to Me
Famous Last Words. . .

A colleague of mine named Larry Kaminer is also an expert in crisis planning, and he once told me something related to preparation. He said, "The enemies of readiness and preparedness are apathy, complacency, and arrogance." Of course, he is correct.

The most common manifestation of these enemies is the thinking that "it will never happen to me. . .and if it does I can deal with it." I've often discussed my "CNN theory" with clients. It's the myth held onto by the business leader who thinks that all that crisis, chaos, and terrible tragedy we see on CNN happens to someone else. I've come to the belief that this is part of human nature. As when we are young and believe we are invincible, the same misplaced confidence arises in us that someone else is the one on television being interviewed, not us. I always remind my clients that those people being interviewed on CNN (or at least, those who are part of a crisis) didn't wake up that morning thinking they would be there.

Dogs seem to have a healthy balance on this issue. They have a strong confidence and high level of boldness. Yet their noses keep them attuned to potential danger. I'm convinced that they are never so arrogant as to believe danger could never strike them, yet not so timid that they aren't literally sticking their noses in places to take a sniff at what's outside.

Do yourself a favor, and it will help you clear this obstacle of the CNN theory. Be bold, confident, and assertive, yet keep in the back of your mind the fact that the only way you can continue to act like this is if you've planned to be ready for anything. It's a form of insurance that doesn't come on a policy and has no premium attached. It's the strategic visioning of someone who isn't so cavalier to believe that "Murphy's Law" won't find him or her. In fact, it's the confident and balanced leader—the Unleashed leader—who makes plans to succeed in the face of any challenge presented.

An Ounce

Saving Time, Money, & Frustration with a Single Ounce

On the spur of the moment one night, my wife and I planned a rare opportunity to share an hour together in Seattle for a date. Barb works in Seattle, and she was planning on meeting our daughter at 6:30 p.m. when Kelli got off work. She asked me to come over early and meet her in the city. I needed to catch the 4:35 p.m. Bainbridge ferry, meet her at the terminal, and then walk into the city for happy hour. For those of you not familiar with a very popular transit system in the Puget Sound, the Washington State Ferries shuttle commuters back and forth across the sound at between thirty to forty-five minutes per crossing. Based on where I live, it's my preferred way to get to Seattle.

After dropping Bella off at home following her veterinarian appointment, I grabbed my sports coat, sprinted out the door, and raced to the ferry from my house. . .about a twenty-five-minute trip. Everything was going swell. I was making all the lights, and based on my keen calculations, would be on the boat with a cool five minutes to spare.

Then it happened. As I approached my final stoplight, a "cautious" driver slowed me down, and I missed the critical light. After an excruciating two minutes, I jetted into the parking lot only to be met by nary a free spot due to a Seattle Sounders playoff match. I found one a distance away that another driver had parked poorly next to, so I had to maneuver to get in. *Ticktock, ticktock.* I frantically bolted down to the pay area and inserted my credit card. The machine toyed with me with a brutally slow, simple transaction. Then I heard, *"This is your thirty second warning!"*

As mentioned, the ferry system is a main thoroughfare for commuters. When they announce "thirty seconds," they mean it!

I grabbed my parking receipt and sprinted down the ramp, counting the seconds in my head, trying to gauge if I would make it. I was hotfooting it like I hadn't in years. Some young guy went racing by me. *When did I get so slow?* As I approached, the gatekeeper started to close the entry gate, and I flew in and it hit my backside (well, almost). The people on deck applauded my herculean effort. I had made the ferry with my Achilles tendon still attached and intact!

I have what is called "Achilles tendonosis." It basically means I have a chronic Achilles challenge and need to be prudent about care. As I sat on the ferry, I stretched it out a bit and "walked it off." After I met Barb in the terminal, we ended up hiking about Seattle and back, all with my Achilles tendon feeling pretty good.

The next morning was a whole different story. While that nagging Achilles had felt okay the rest of the evening, that next morning came with it *screaming* at me. I struggled to stand up and was barely able to walk. I knew my trip back into Seattle for a full-day retreat with a new client was going to be more painful for me than it was for them! My smirking daughter offered to fetch my dad's old cane. *Funny.* As the old 10cc song from the 1970s exclaims, "The things we do for love. . . "

It was easy for me to blame others for my painful limp. The other drivers, the stoplight, and the pay machine could all be held culpable, right? No, it was my fault. Had I simply planned just a little bit better, I would have arrived sooner and gently sauntered onto the boat.

Too many of you are limping into your days uncertain and unprepared for a crisis. Calamity doesn't send a calling card. In my Achilles story, I was negligent in many areas, specifically with poor planning and preparation, which resulted in my sprinting to catch my ride and doing damage to an already vulnerable body part. How much better can you be if you are preventing crises from happening though your activities and behaviors? I could have left earlier and prevented the pain. What are you not doing that might prevent your crisis from ever even occurring?

Organizational Amnesia
How to Avoid It Before They Walk out the Door

A few years ago, I received a phone call from a person representing the facilities unit for a United States Navy installation. A colleague at another installation where I had done leadership training had referred her to me.

Laura knew exactly what she wanted. She said to me, "We have a serious pending issue because over 50 percent of our workforce will be eligible to retire in five years. We are concerned that a whole bunch of valuable knowledge is going to walk out the door without our having captured it."

This was very proactive thinking. I was hired by that facility and have since been doing ongoing projects and trainings with them. They have kept that challenge front and center in their thinking. What about you?

The Baby Boomer generation (1946–1964) is quickly hitting a time frame where *retiring* will happen in waves. I italicize *retiring* because I don't think they are all just shutting down work and sipping iced tea from their front porches. I believe that they are phasing out of jobs and careers that they've toiled at for decades and are seeking new adventures and opportunities. The result for businesses will be a loss of the vital information that resides in their brains. If that intellectual capital isn't snared properly by businesses, then it might be lost forever.

I call this process "organizational amnesia." It's a subtle loss of intellectual capital and "smarts" as people leave an organization for any reason. However, when it's more than just a ripple as people "age out," then it can quickly turn into a loss of memory for the company, an amnesia that can't be reversed. This is a crisis for companies and many don't even know it exists. Luckily for you, you're reading this now! My client in the Navy understands it, and so should you.

For the sake of clarity for the rest of this section, let's do a little defining. From here on out, *veterans* will mean your long-standing employees who have the intellectual capital and are on the verge (inside of five years) of retiring from your company. The term *teammate* refers only to someone who isn't a veteran. They might be *rookies* (in their first two years) in your organization, or they might have been with you ten to fifteen years, but they have a lot of time left to play.

I suggest that organizational amnesia and its consequences can be prevented with a little forethought and action. This is my **Super 7 Approach** to averting a crisis of loss of intellectual firepower:

1. **Begin a Mentoring Program.** This concept has been discussed in depth earlier in the book, so I won't spend an inordinate amount of time discussing it here. The key element here is that your veterans mentor those most likely to take over roles and responsibilities. It's often easiest to do with rookies; however, as teammates advance in your ranks, they may need that more formalized training.

2. **Hold Team-Building Workshops.** This concept revolves around a collaborative and collective sharing of thoughts and ideas. I recall sales meetings where I learned a lot from veterans

just by listening to their conversations. This can be enhanced for you if you simply make it the priority of the workshop.

3. **Incentivize Veterans.** There are many ways to incentivize people and money is only one way. That being said, incentives work well when trying to glean information from one person and transfer it to another. This might be part of your mentoring or other workshops. In any event, your veterans have gained knowledge though their investments of time, talent, skills, experiences, and bloodied noses. Paying them back as a "return on investment" to help others isn't a bad idea.

4. **Write.** Have your veterans start writing down their processes, their contact information (whatever lies outside of your standard contact management system), and other components of their jobs that they might actually take for granted. Have them start early on this process. In fact, a good idea is to have everyone take part. This accomplishes two things. First, it gets all the information that is important to your company out into one place. Second, you never know when a teammate or a rookie will leave the company. You don't want to lose their "smarts" with their departure either.

5. **Use Audio/Video.** Audio and video have become very easy to create and to store. I have clients who create podcasts, broadcasts, and webinars. Record all of these. You have smart people creating interesting and valuable information while they are working for you. Store all of this and maybe even use it when training others to do the same.

6. **Interview.** Spend time interviewing veterans on processes, strategies, techniques, and tactics. You might even consider videotaping them, at the very least, record their words for posterity and future reference.

7. **Create a Library.** It's easier than ever with technology to create a virtual library of information. Everything that I've noted above about training, interviews, documents, and videos can go in this

library. You must ultimately capture and store all the powerful intellectual capital that resides in your company.

Of note: you might find yourself in the position of being one of those with "smarts" that need to be captured. As a leader, or even the boss, you too have scads of important information that need to be gleaned. In the process of avoiding the crisis of organizational amnesia, don't "forget" yourself!

A Captain Jack Extra Point
The Nose Knows

We dogs tend not to overthink things. After all, if we do, we run the danger of talking ourselves out of fun things. That's a human condition. What we do is boldly go where we want and be prepared to deal with adversity. That's what our nose knows. . .

Our noses are our super-power. Too bad yours are just large without any real power. We can sense perils and risks. And to that end, we know what to do when we come across it. We've figured out that whole "fight or flight" mentality that psychologists on the human side wrote about. We know when either is most appropriate. That being said, we stay out of a lot of predicaments because we anticipate in order to prevent. Our nose lets us know early enough to make decisions.

Humans can do the same—just not with their noses! You get to use experiences. I don't always remember what I did yesterday, but you all remember what happened years ago. Your ability to recall experiences can be beneficial to you in planning. That way, you might be able to actually avoid and prevent, and then better deal with your own "fight or flight" issues when they come up.

Bottom line: you need to create your own nose for risk and peril. You can use that nose to your advantage if you just smell.

Just saying. . .
Captain Jack

The Mitigation Motif

WINNING THE BATTLE WHEN YOU'RE UP TO YOUR ELBOWS IN IT

I am somewhat of a *heat seeker*. Barb has accused me of inexplicably gravitating towards crisis and chaos. In the roles I assume and the projects I take on, invariably there is some level of crisis percolating (or about to erupt). Sitting still and being quiet hasn't been in my nature. It's one of the many things Barb is exceptionally good at and why we balance each other well. A quiet mind, even just once in a while, is a requisite for getting out of a crisis. It's what I recommend to my consulting clients, and it's what I recommend for you. This chapter is about ensuring that no crisis is fatal. It's about getting out of any crisis, however you define that. Let's see how we can eradicate the noise and gain a quiet mind in the midst of chaos.

When I coached high school basketball in the early 2000s, I incorporated a drill I'd learned at a Nike coaching clinic from a workshop given by one of their esteemed college coaches. It's called, simply, "Situations."

The concept is to simulate end-of-game situations so as to be prepared for them when they naturally occur. Decisions made in real time are usually poor. I wanted us to be ready for anything. This daily drill involved me choosing some situation concerning a close game with a short amount of time remaining. We would then put the time up on the clock and play a "real" game, and afterward, assess our effort and outcome.

Example: We are down by three points with forty-five seconds left in the game. It's the opponent's ball underneath our basket. Each team has one timeout left. Both teams are in the double bonus for free throws. Play!

I would take one team, and my assistant would take the other. We would take turns playing on both sides. The kids loved the drill because it brought a reality and a challenge to what could be dull practices. It gave me the opportunity, as their coach, to provide valuable "stage time" to my players. In essence, we were practicing how to use fire extinguishers for different kinds of fires.

In my consulting career, I've taken this concept of "situations" to a strategic crisis management realm to help my clients be prepared for calamity. Dealing with and responding to crises—both small and large—is an executive function, just like it is for the head coach on a basketball team. Readying yourself and your team for any situation can also prepare you and your team in a crisis.

Are You Ready?

"Are you ready?"

This may be the most asked question known to man.

- Are you ready for your test?
- Are you ready to play?
- Are you ready for that big sales call?
- Are you ready for dinner?
- Are you ready to meet with the board?
- Are you ready for the game?
- Are you ready to go?

You get my point. The question *"Are you ready?"* is a significant one because our careers and lives are much smoother and happier when the answer is a resounding and confidant, **YES**. You always feel better when you can boldly answer in the affirmative, don't you? You are fearless; you stand taller; you're more poised and prepared. You bubble over with the assurance that, whatever you were getting "ready" for, you've done all you can and you will not fail.

If the answer is NO, it's a different vibe. It's evident in your posture and your voice. There is hesitation, concern, stress, anxiety, and lack of confidence. If this is a weighty matter (e.g., job interview, final exam, or sales presentation), it only exacerbates these feelings of inadequacy. You may just find yourself saying, "I should have prepared better."

I still vividly remember the day my daughter Kelli and I picked up Captain Jack. It was July 1, 2008. This spunky one-year-old puppy had been found wandering about a neighborhood, and nobody had claimed him. I can still see his wistful little face as he sat in a cage with a dilapidated stuffed bear next to him. Of course, Kelli fell in love with him at first sight. I figured, *What the heck? This should be easy. He's just a little guy.*

We were in the market for another dog. Our first family dog, Blondie, had passed away seven months earlier, and our remaining dog, Charlie, wanted a friend. For companionship's sake, we preferred having two dogs. Kelli took the lead "project manager" role, and she discovered Jack on the Humane Society website. So here we were—all ready to bring him home. And then came the question. . .

"Are you ready for a Jack Russell terrier?"

The nice lady at the front desk stopped me prior to my writing a check and asked if I'd filled out the "special" paperwork. I hadn't. She made me go back to Jack's cage and get the form that was hanging on the front. I saw Captain Jack looking somewhat forlornly at me, as if giving his last "pitch" to go home with us. The paperwork was pretty straightforward. It explained that Jack Russell terriers were the most returned dogs to Humane Society shelters. Prospective owners like us would think that all Jack Russell terriers (JRTs for us *connoisseurs* of the breed) behaved like Eddie from the hit television show *Frasier*. While Eddie certainly was a JRT, the shelter made it very clear that the breed is quite energetic and that readiness for this onslaught of intensity was advised.

The final words were the most conspicuous. This shelter had a NO RETURN policy on JRTs. Once you walked out the door, he or she was yours.

As I now more deliberately ambled back to the front desk, I started pondering the question *Am I ready for this dog?*

I knew I was too far down the line to back out. My confidence was declining because it had been a long time since I had dealt with an ambitious puppy. We consummated the deal, and Captain Jack came home with us. Immediately upon arrival at his new home, he displayed the personality that the breed is noted for. . .and then some. Captain Jack was "in the house" and had no plans of leaving!

We weren't ready for this new vitality. While we quickly fell in love with him and would never return him in spite of his precocious nature (or maybe even because of it), we made many mistakes. These mistakes led to him escaping (many times) and us having to chase him down, incessant digging, obnoxious barking, and a multitude of mischievous behaviors. In the end, it took longer than necessary to introduce him into the family.

When you're not ready for what's coming for you, the same results will occur: the process may be more painful, cost you more money, and be more of a nuisance. As we might have been better served to have done research on JRTs to be better prepared, you can do your own due diligence to be more willing to boldly answer YES to the question of being ready to lead others effectively in a crisis situation.

Follow Me
How to Lead in Crisis

The most important characteristic that a leader can have in a stressful situation is the formidable ability to be *nimble*.

Nimble is defined by me this way: The capacity to make weighty decisions quickly, to turn those decisions into immediate action, and to be prepared to deal with the results or consequences of that decision. And then rinse and repeat. . .

We are certainly creatures of habit and often violently evade change at all costs. While having a regular process can be important, it can also sabotage opportunity.

If you were having lunch at the next table over from my ninety-year-old mother and me when she was alive and at her assisted living community, you might have overheard this conversation:

Mom: You're my favorite.

Me: Your favorite what? [I'm her only child, so I was curious.]

Mom: My favorite nephew.

Me [with a chuckle]: Well, that's fine, but I'm your son!

Mom [with her own chuckle]: Oh. . .that's right!

This conversation would have been unthinkable about three years earlier. My mom had been fully capable and living on her own with my father. In the next two and a half years, my father developed bladder cancer, they moved to an assisted living facility, he died and she moved in with us for two years, and finally, we moved her to a memory care facility as her dementia progressively evolved. Her life changed and so did ours, seemingly overnight. We were forced to make decisions with a whole new reality and time frame while at the same time our own beliefs around aging and mortality were changing. We experienced how rapidly health can decline, the suddenly excessive cost of health care, and the necessity of making changes in the blink of an eye. It forced us to be *nimble*.

Mitigating crises requires nimbleness. It's one thing to prepare for any type of crisis, and it's quite a different thing to have to make decisions in the heat and emotion of the battle. This chapter will give you tools to be calm in the face of the storm in order to make good decisions that will affect both your short- and long-range plans and operations.

In the very beginning of my first year coaching basketball, and before I'd even had my first practice, one of my early mentors asked if he could impart some words of wisdom. Steve Frease was a veteran coach at North Kitsap High School. He had experience as a head coach and assistant coach in many sports, and at this time, was a highly successful baseball coach at the school. Of course, I was not only willing to listen to him, I was anxious to get his advice.

Steve said, "Dan, you can't control a lot of things as coach. One thing you can be certain of, though, is this: you will be forced to endure at least three crises every year. Some years there will be more, but even in the best of them, you will have at least three. How you respond and manage them will determine the year you have. And I'm not talking about just wins and losses. I mean how fun the year will be for your players and you."

Boy, was Coach Frease ever right. Many years we had numerous crises, and some years we just had the three of them. They all came at different times and without warning. His advice saved our season, and me, on more than one occasion. That's why I share it with you.

We all will suffer crises. They will differ somewhat based on whether you're dealing with them as an individual or as the owner/executive of a business. The term *crisis* is defined differently depending on whom you're asking. Here is my definition:

Crisis is in the eye of the beholder. Crisis has no maximum or minimum on consequences. It is solely judged by the adverse effect it has on an individual, a family, a business, or a community. Crisis involves loss or damage to money, trust, assets, people, reputation, and/or brand. It is easily gotten into and usually more challenging to get out of. In the end, it's a part of life and should be expected and prepared for. In every situation, how we deal with crisis will determine our success, happiness, and future.

Crisis is too amorphous to place in a box. In my role as a consultant, I work with business leaders to help them be more prepared. Unfortunately, too many of them consider crisis as "the big one." All too often, it's not the fires, floods, and earthquakes that are the enemies because these are usually well-prepared for. Most often, it's the small things, which aren't always considered crises, that cause the real challenges. Here are a few crises examples that are easily missed because they exist below the waterline, unseen and uncontemplated:

- Poor morale caused by bad hiring decisions
- Loss of promotion because you didn't ask
- Loss of opportunity because you failed to act in time
- Loss of vital information because you didn't have proper redundancy
- Loss of money because you chose not to get identity theft protection
- Loss of use of equipment because you chose not to fix something in a timely manner
- Loss of key employees because you chose not to listen to concerns
- Loss of your best clients because you allowed relationships to drift into apathy

These are all under your control. Certainly, there are many crises that are outside of your control including:

- Weather
- Human error
- Accidents (human and mechanical)
- Criminal acts
- Someone else's bad judgments or behaviors
- Poor timing
- Someone else's preconceived notions or individual agendas
- Bad luck

As a leader there are three things you need to do guide your company though stormy waters:

1. Have a "positivity over panic" mentality
2. Be able to make tough decisions quickly and commit
3. Communicate well

Positivity Over Panic—One of the areas I wish I had been better at when coaching high school girls was not looking panicked. I was a pretty emotional coach and tried to use that to motivate. Unfortunately, when the game was tight and I wanted poise, I projected panic because I looked like a madman on the sideline. While that might often work for male athletes, female athletes drew a different inference. The results were that they picked up on an emotion (panic), which wasn't really there. I actually had confidence, but how I projected made it seem like I didn't. It's the old "perception is reality" deal. I wish I had remained calmer, projected a more composed demeanor (even if inside I wasn't composed) and exuded confident positivity. I truly believe it would have made a difference in their play, and even added a few more victories.

You must also exude positivity in the face of adversity. The next section will cover strategies and techniques for decision-making. For now, own the reality that you will set the perception for your company, your organization, or simply your own department when the going gets tough. I wish I could have seen myself and adjusted accordingly. You need to have that invisible "mirror" available to you. How you look, your demeanor, and your calm will go a long way in pushing out positive vibes when they are most needed. You might just be the only face of your little world at that moment. How do you want to look?

Commitment—Smart and savvy people make quick decisions all the time. Emotion is the engine that entices people to movement. Making decisions doesn't require reams of research or a committee. All that is required is a good sense of timing, need, and applicability. . .and then commitment.

My daughter Kelli was recently searching for a rental home after she got her job in Seattle. She and a friend uncovered what appeared to be a good opportunity. The rental was in good shape, although in an older neighborhood. Because the rental market was so dynamic, Kelli and her friend didn't have too much time to ruminate on their decision. Within three days, they made a quick visit, asked key questions, checked their budget, and then took the leap of faith. They committed to their decision. While every box wasn't checked, nor every question answered, they had enough information to make an informed decision. Timing dictated it be made quickly. While something might someday pop up and make the decision seem bad, the reality is that most likely they will continue to be pleased with their choice.

You will be forced to make decisions that you aren't prepared for during a crisis. However, your experience in life and business will allow you to take in information, ask key questions, and check your budget. You will make a decision with the information you have and (here is the important part) make a commitment and buy into it. Your team will follow a leader who makes a bold commitment, rather than an indecisive one. You can't be overly worried about the outcome because you can't control everything. What you can control is your decision and your commitment to making it.

Communicate—Communication is a constant theme in this book and in most books that discuss leadership. You will be watched by everyone—employees, customers, the media, and your business community. The words you choose and their delivery method will be critical to gaining support when fighting a crisis.

Communication skills require practice. The best method is role-playing with peers. Take a cue from my example of coaching "Situations." Create your own, and practice how you will communicate. You can role-play talking to your crisis team, your employees, your investors, the media, and your customers and clients. Learn from it, and practice what you learn.

Here's a good role-play example: Take three people and form a "team." One person plays the part of the leader communicating in a crisis situation. The second is the "audience." That means the employee, the manager, a reporter, etc. The third person is the observer. He or she watches and offers observations about the role-play so both of the other parties can focus on their roles. After one is done, switch situations and roles. Each person will have the very powerful opportunity to be in every role, thus helping each other maximize learning.

The Running Clock
Decision Making Basics for Leaders

Once a crisis hits, it's as if you're on a running clock. Remember my basketball coaching example earlier? Your clock may not only be running, but you might also be out of timeouts!

Regardless of the crisis, you have to have a plan for dealing with it. I suggest to my clients that it be as simple as possible. Here is my three-step process to keeping a quiet mind in chaos:

Step 1—Stop and Assess: Ask one question—"How bad is it?" Whatever the situation, there is a level of "badness," and you need to determine it. More often than you might think, "How bad is it?" isn't as dire as you might imagine. The majority of the decisions you are making (unless you're a brain surgeon, paramedic, or jungle guide) don't involve life and death. They may not even involve immediate financial concerns. This process takes slowing everything down, breathing, and candidly assessing the urgency and "danger" of your crisis.

Having a quiet mind allows you to think. Even if you have to remove yourself from others just for a few minutes, you can literally slow yourself down. This creates better focus and decisions. I mentioned earlier in the book that Edgar Martinez and the best hitters in baseball can actually see the seams of the baseball being thrown at them at over ninety miles per hour. They've slowed their minds and have extreme focus. You have to get into a slow-motion mentality to see the problem and begin deliberating on what the next move is. This is an intentional approach, which needs to be practiced.

Extra Point: The best way to handle this is in advance. If you can identify your crises and make decisions before decisions need to be made, you're far better off. Most families have a gathering spot outside the house in case the home must be evacuated. Ours was under the only streetlight on the corner. We all knew it in advance, so we wouldn't need to be reminded. If you run a business, you must have a crisis plan. If you're an executive or manager, you must communicate the plan to your people. If you're an individual, you must know how you are prepared to respond in the case of an emergency. In any of these roles, not doing so is just negligent and puts others in harm's way.

You can help yourself immeasurably by forming a team. The team should consist of various roles and responsibilities. I would make sure that my human resources director, technology director, insurance liaison (or broker), sales manager, and operations manager, at the very least, were part of the team. Someone needs to be charged with the job of Crisis Commander. Depending on your leadership role, it might be you!

There isn't enough room in this book to go through all scenarios. That's another book in and of itself! What you do need is to ensure that your company develops a plan that is communicated and practiced. Crises don't call ahead. Good leaders are prepared for them.

Step 2—Make a Decision: Recall that I stated earlier that smart people make decisions quickly. You've assessed how bad the situation is (or isn't). Now you must weigh the pros and cons on possible decisions. Each decision has an upside and a downside. If you can honesty appraise which one is best, then commit and go with it. If time is of the essence, your window is smaller. If it's not, ask for some help, but don't overanalyze. You are smarter than you think, and people are looking for a decisive leader. In almost all cases I can think of (again, outside of life and death), your decisions aren't going to change the course of Western civilization. While they may be of great importance in a crisis, don't put too much pressure on yourself. Think clearly, work off your plan, commit, and go.

I remember clearly the day I decided to quit my job and start my consulting practice in 2005. While this might not seem like a "crisis situation," as an individual looking at jumping ship from a steady paycheck, with two daughters about to graduate high school, *crisis* would be one of the words that came to mind if my plan didn't work!

The idea of becoming a consultant had come to me in a quiet moment sitting by myself (quiet mind). This decision involved the security of my family financially and emotionally. I did research online and found an insurance consultant in Maine by the name of Scott Simmonds. I called Scott to ask some questions, and he was kind enough to provide some answers. He also told me he had a mentor program for $3,500. My decision was really at its crossroads (time to stop and assess). I had pretty much all the information I needed. It was time to evaluate the upside and the downside (and of course, consult with my family). It took twenty-four hours. I made the decision to move forward and committed to paying Scott the fee to get started. The whole process took three days.

Remember, crisis looks different for everyone. Your crisis may simply be an opportunity that involves risk, or it could be physical (property damage). No matter what it is, the process remains the same when it comes to quickly making a decision.

Step 3—Communicate: This is the most overlooked in the entire crisis process. Lack of communication, miscommunication, and misinformation only add to any crisis. Sometimes, a lack of communication, or a miscommunication, causes crisis all by itself!

Because of that, it gets its very own section. . .next!

When the Going Gets Tough
Crisis Communications Strategies for Leaders

Communication is critical before, during, and after a crisis. This could involve your employees, or it could involve your family. In the end, everyone needs to be on the same page, and you might be the nexus of that communication trail. When I made the decision to leave my job, I didn't wait long after hiring Scott as my mentor. Two days later, I met with my boss and I fully communicated the details. Within a week, we had determined how we would communicate to staff and clients. It allowed the transition to be better for everyone.

Here are a few best practices around communicating in crisis situations:

- **Be Honest.** Sounds easy, yet all too often we see "dishonesty" in crisis communications in the form of untruths and omissions. Nothing good ever comes from that. While there may be information that must be kept private, just saying that is honest enough.

- **Avoid "No Comment."** Maybe the worst phrase ever invented to avoid questions. It implies that you are trying to hide something. It's much better to say, "We don't have answers right now. We understand the uncertainty can cause anxiety, and we are committed to getting those answers as quickly as possible."

- **Tell the Right People First.** People don't like surprises, especially business partners, executives, investors, and spouses. If you're in a business situation that requires that your executives, managers, and most critical people know about it before anyone else, then tell them first. The last thing you want is a subordinate of theirs asking them questions about a crisis they weren't aware of and embarrassing them. There is an organizational chain of communication. Identify it and use it.

- **Be Empathetic.** Most crises involve the need for empathy. Even if it's good news (e.g., me leaving to start my own practice), there are people who might be adversely affected. Showing genuine empathy and concern for all the potential fears and discomfort of others is not only good business, it's being a good human. As an example, a crisis in your business might cause concern over job security. Families and their financial and emotional health are at risk, and emotions can run high. This is no time to be "corporate." If you think of humans first, you're more likely to be trusted and followed.

- **Avoid the "One and Done."** Have you ever been in a situation where you received an immediate wave of information at the beginning of some crisis, and then never again? Crises often have a life of their own. It's important to stay consistent and persistent on your messaging and communications. Back in the mid-1990s, Odwalla had a terrible crisis in their juices with an *E. coli* outbreak. Their CEO was brilliant in his response, both immediately and for a lengthy time afterwards. In fact, in the days before widespread Internet, Odwalla created a special website and online presence to keep distributors informed. The CEO's commitment to open and ongoing communication probably saved the company from demise after a huge and highly publicized debacle.

- **Get Help.** It's important to have the right messenger. If it's not you (recall assessing your own strengths, talents, and skills?), then find someone either internally or externally to be that messenger. Internally, many companies find someone to be their "voice"—someone who is gifted and talented in communications (both written and spoken). Externally, there are companies that are experts in public relations and crisis management. It's crucial to not only get the word out, but to do it well. If you're not the person for that job, find someone who is.

- **Exude Positivity.** Have you seen this one before? You don't have to be a cheerleader, nor insult the intelligence of the people you're communicating to with a false sense of reality. However, you can still portray that the sky is not falling, that you and the company are resilient, that you have great people, and that all is being done to deal swiftly with the situation. In a crisis involving a company and employees, always remember that people will be in fear for their jobs and future. Being positive in the face of crisis will signify hope and encouragement. As a leader, that's what you need to offer.

Final Thoughts: Eighteen holes of golf offer many opportunities to deal with crisis. Some are out of our control, and others are of our own doing. Having a basic plan and having practiced for it (both mentally and skill-wise) makes dealing with these crises easier. You need to own a sand wedge and have used it a few times in order to escape a sand trap.

As you've read, I'm an avid golfer. I believe golf is one of the most accurate metaphors we have for life. Over the course of eighteen holes, a golfer will encounter both lofty "highs" and heartbreaking "lows." And the majority of holes will be neither. To be a good golfer, you must be prepared to deal with those lows, or else they can ruin your game.

Life has plenty of sand traps awaiting us on our journey. We need the proper tools and requisite practice to be resilient. Unlike golf, our ability to be calm and decisive in crisis affects many other people, like family, employees and their families, customers, business partners, investors, and the community. While the stakes are often high, the best leaders respond with composure and coolness, even as chaos may be all around them. In order to be truly Unleashed, you need to add these clubs to your bag!

A Captain Jack Extra Point
Instinctual Damage (or Bladder) Control

Dan talks a lot about sports. In just this chapter, he's blathered on about basketball and golf. I often wonder if he does that because he can't think up his own examples. Or maybe, he just watches too much sports!

Believe it or not, we dogs also have to deal with crisis and have no sports analogies to provide. We can run out of water when our humans forget to fill our bowls. We can encounter a rogue rabbit trying to gain access to our yard. And the worst is when we are stuck in the house all day and our access to the exit is blocked as our bladder fills.

When the bladder fills too much and you can't get out, what are you going to do? You just go and deal with the issues later. It's better than the alternative. We consider the pros and the cons, or as Dan says, upsides and downsides, and make the best decision we can with the information we have. Simple.

Humans think too much. I guess what I should say is that you overthink things. We trust implicitly our sense of intuition and instinct. While you may not be as intuitive as a dog, you still have some intuition. Use it. When the going gets tough, it takes more than just saying "the tough get going." You'd better be going somewhere, or else you will find more trouble. Make sure you use your instinct and intuition, and then trust in them like we trust in ours. You will probably find that you get out of trouble much quicker that way, even if you have to occasionally pee on a floor.

Just saying. . .
Captain Jack

Thriving

HOW TO TURN CALAMITY INTO OPPORTUNITY. . . FAST

The conclusion of the last chapter sets up my next statement. Golf is analogous to life. It's a remarkable journey filled with joy, charm, crisis, and serendipity spread out over eighteen holes. Some holes are easy, and some are brutally harsh. *Fair* isn't a word that has a place on the golf course because golf isn't "fair." Neither is the journey we are on, be it in our business or in life.

In golf, one faces an assortment of "approaches." Often the shot into the green is clear, making both opportunity and threats easily visible. Other times, golfers face "blind" shots, where they can't see what lies beyond due to the terrain. This is where they often must swing on faith and trust alone. There is rarely (at least, in my game) a round that goes by without a crisis of some sort rearing its ugly head. I'm always met with opportunities to make a "save" and "recover." Funny how that sounds a lot like being a leader.

I remember well a particular hole on a dusky night when I was a teenager. My buddy Mike and I were undoubtedly the last people on the course since nobody else was in sight. It was a summer evening, and when you're seventeen years old and can play unlimited golf on a country club course in a small town, you play golf until you can't walk or see anymore.

We were playing Hole #8 at the Whidbey Golf and Country Club in

Oak Harbor, WA, and were soon approaching the latter of the two options I presented. Hole #8 is a dogleg right with a huge man-made lake to the right of the tee. It guards a sloped green. The only real shot is to hit a mid-range wood or an iron down the middle of the fairway and then approach over the water with a short club. For me, it was a 4-iron down the middle and a 9-iron to the hole. As golf holes go, this was actually a pretty simple, uncomplicated hole. I was a much better player back then (daily play will do that), and I considered this a hole I could chase a birdie on. That summer night, I didn't know exactly how right I was!

The chief inhabitant of the lake was a colossal white swan. While magnificent to look at, this bad boy was one mean dude. I believe that he felt like all these knuckleheaded golfers were encroaching on his territory. He was well-known to all of us at the club as a cantankerous beast with a nasty temper.

That night the Great White (as we dubbed him) was strolling around the green looking for his evening dessert of roots and tubers. After a solid tee shot, I hit a sweet 9-iron into the green and landed it above the hole about nine feet away. I was in range for that birdie. Mike hit his shot on the putting surface as well, and as we approached the green, an unusual thing happened. The Great White had jumped up on the green and waddled over to my ball. He was closely inspecting it as if he thought it was some sort of egg. I yelled at him, "Get away from my ball!" He either understood me or realized that this golf ball was not food. Suddenly, with an indignant air, he kicked my ball down the slope of the green! The ball raced past the hole, over the fringe, and plopped gently into the hazard of about a half-inch of water and mud.

I was furious. I hollered a profanity-laced outburst and stormed to the green. The Great White, true to his surly demeanor, bellowed back at me while flailing his enormous wings. At that moment, I realized that this guy could inflict some serious damage, and I wasn't willing to get into an altercation with him.

The next question raised was what the proper ruling was. Mike thought that since the swan was part of the course, I had to play the ball where it was lying in the water. I said the swan was an interloper and I could replace the ball. Ultimately, I played both shots. The ball out of the water and mud was a little trickier. I was able to extricate the ball out of that mess and onto the green and made a bogey. My original ball was played at par. To this day, I still have great debates with my golfing buddies (especially one persistent pal named Jim) about the proper ruling, and it may never be cleared up to my satisfaction. So it is with golf stories. . .

Sometimes, an unforeseen "swan" occurs that you'd never imagine could possibly happen in your business. What seems to be a simple day may suddenly turn perilous. The likelihood of my ball being kicked off the green by a big white swan was never considered when I was teeing off. As you traverse your own business "golf course," you will encounter strange things. Very often, you will be forced to do what I did. . .hit it out of the hazard. I was able to salvage a bogey rather than blow up with a really high score, which would have only exacerbated my indignation. You have to find ways to avoid the triple bogeys in your organization by minimizing the consequences of crisis. That way, you are assured your best possible score at the conclusion of your round.

The past chapters have discussed preventing calamity and mitigating the effects based on your leadership. Now we have to thrive out of calamity. In my story about the swan, I actually thrived through the experience, even though I didn't know it at the time. These were my lessons:

- I learned how to overcome a little adversity. In fact, that was a constant theme in my golf game, yet this situation was so out of the ordinary, it forced me to think outside of the box. *Are you ever forced to make decisions on issues that you've never dealt with prior, or even considered as a possibility?*

- I had never attempted to hit a ball out of the water. There's a first time for everything, right? It's not a shot one would normally practice, and when you face it for real, there are no mulligans (do-overs). *When was the last time you had to work through a strange (and maybe once-in-a-lifetime) crisis, knowing you had never prepared for it?*

- I had to compromise. Mike and I never really played for kicks and giggles. There was always a side game going on, and that was part of the fun. In the end, we both were firm on our ruling, so I played both balls as a provisional situation until we got an unbiased ruling. *Have you ever had to put your ego aside for compromising's sake? How hard is it for you to stand down in the face of adversity and disagreement?*

These little lessons learned in even the smallest of crises all add up and build your ability to find opportunity in the darkest of clouds. We've all heard of silver linings, right? The silver linings and learning moments all are there for you as opportunities to thrive as long as you're paying attention.

Every Crisis Has Opportunity
Can You Find It?

There have been segments in this book where I've written on the concept of being in the moment. The reason I can write and speak so openly about its importance is because I've struggled most of my life with this concept. It wasn't until I began working closely with Alan Weiss and his community of world-class consultants that I began to identify tools and techniques for being in the moment.

One of the reasons I love golf is because I'm forced to apply this concept. I tell Barb that playing golf is good for my mental acuity, business welfare, and physical fitness. While I'm quite sure her eye-rolling wasn't deliberate, I'm not sure she is buying it. But I do. . .here is why:

When I play golf now, I have to focus solely on the next shot. That means blocking out the last missed putt or great drive. That means not thinking about the next hole or what numbers I need to have to post a low score. The focus is on that next shot and swing.

I taught my basketball players this concept and encouraged them to master it. It's the "next play" mentality that allows you to never dwell on either the good or the bad in the past and to only use them for experience. That's where opportunity is hiding. And that's why we often miss it.

Take this moment to be reflective. Think back on something you considered a crisis situation for you in your business. Was it a lost client? Was it losing a key employee to a competitor? Was it a fire that damaged your building and contents? Was it an economic downturn that saw your business suffer for two to three years?

Now be honest and assess what you learned from the event. For each situation, the lesson will be different. The biggest mistake we make is not stopping and examining what we learned. We simply move past having endured the trauma but don't look to find how and why we did it, and what good we can make from it.

The most common denominator in overcoming adversity is resilience. Lack of resilience is also unfortunately the thing that will keep you from being Unleashed in business and in life. That means you'd better find a way to be resilient over and over again. That's the topic of our next section.

The Resiliency Dogma
Can You Take a Punch?

Losing a Super Bowl is brutal and painful. When you lose it the way the Seattle Seahawks did in 2015 to the New England Patriots, it's even worse. For the players and coaches, the organization, and the fans, it's still excruciating.

In the span of about thirty "real-time" seconds from the point when Marshawn Lynch was tackled on the one-yard line to the fateful interception by Patriots cornerback Malcolm Butler, we all went from the jubilation of winning the Super Bowl to losing. Cruel.

The Seattle Seahawks and their fans basically took a brutal punch to the gut.

Now I understand that this wasn't the most compelling crisis that was occurring around the world at the time. There was a measles outbreak in the United States, horrific terrorist activity around the globe, and a winter storm was pummeling the Midwest and East Coast. These were far weightier problems.

However, for the players and members of their organization, football is their livelihood. Just as you and I go about our jobs and careers, this is their "business." That not only includes high-salaried players and coaches, it also means the office and support staff in the building. So losing is the equivalent to your company being "sucker punched" and having the entire organization in crisis-mode. They will need to determine if they can take a punch. (Note that as I write this book, the next season has yet to begin. We will soon find out together!)

My question for you is ***Can you take a punch?***

The Seahawks have to answer this question as an organization. The culture, the churn of players and coaches, and the overall mindset must stay resilient. There will be hurt feelings in the locker room. There is likely to be drama regarding new contracts offered and others not offered. There will be that lingering feeling of opportunity lost that never goes away. Leadership and communication will be critical to their ability to take a punch and stand back up.

The same is true for you in business and in your personal life. You must not only be able to take a punch, but also to get up and be better.

There are two important aspects to this resiliency. **The first is physical.** These are a few questions you will need to consider and answer:

- Do you have *processes and redundancies* in place to overcome a physical disaster like a fire, flood, hurricane, earthquake, or loss of power?
- Is your insurance adequate to *replace and repair* property and financial loss in the past, present, and future?
- Do you have a plan for *staying open* in the interim?
- Can you get your hands on vital equipment, inventory, and people immediately and *cause as little disruption* as possible?

- Can you and your employees *evacuate safely* in the case of extreme emergency?

These are all questions that good business leaders ask and that they set up strategies and contingencies for in advance. You will find many more to consider as an Unleashed leader. This is where you take this book and expand its value by taking action.

The second aspect is more challenging and more important. **The second is emotional.**

Resiliency is easier when fixing property—homes, equipment, buildings, computers. Fixing the emotional side is harder. Here are examples:

- Loss of confidence in the organization from both internal and external partners (employees and customers).
- Depression (may be from a leadership level, an employee morale level, or simply a personal issue in dealing with crisis).
- Distraction (chaos, uncertainty, and other "moving parts" can easily distract attention and focus).
- Fear. Plain and simple fear can be both a motivator and an obstacle to moving forward.
- Sense of loss. This is often overlooked and dismissed in business.
- Uncertainty. See *fear* again.

Unleashed leaders understand three important things about this second form of resiliency:

I. It is a process, is often painful, and takes time and patience. We all like to fix things quickly. Emotional resiliency requires basic (and often advanced) levels of grief, understanding, and perspective. Emotional resiliency can't be rushed, only lightened.

2. It requires constant communication from the top down. Candid, real, and transparent communication. The answer may be "We don't know yet. . . " or "We are going to do the best we can. . . " People understand this level of honesty. Nobody likes to feel they are being patronized, lied to, or missing information

that affects them and their families.

3. It requires trust. Sometimes, in crisis, trust is lost, or at least, damaged. In order to rebuild trust, you must enhance organizational culture. This is always best done when there is no crisis happening. This makes building trust and culture Job #1.

Bottom line: Everyone has to take a punch now and then. Sometimes, it might be right in front of us, and other times it might be a sucker punch that comes flying in from behind. Regardless, resiliency is about fighting through the pain and discomfort, seeking out solutions that benefit the greatest good, and thriving out of crisis.

Can you take a punch?

Thriving or Existing
The Difference Will Be Defining

There is a huge difference between thriving and merely existing. This comment may seem overly simplistic, and it probably is. However, in practice it can be hard to tell.

Leadership isn't intrinsic. It's a skill, and more than that, a mindset. Unleashed leadership takes your mindset to a different level. In order to be a leader who thrives, and in turn, whose team and organization thrives, a few things must be in place.

Let's begin with a couple of definitions. In order to understand how to thrive out of any crisis, conundrum, or conflict, we need to better understand the terms *existing* and *thriving*.

Existing is surviving a calamity and then consciously or unconsciously staying even or declining to come out of it.

I've written about my Achilles tendonosis earlier and the physical challenges the injury presented. As an active person and a frequent traveler, the Achilles injury and consequent symptoms were a minor crisis. Just surviving the injury through rest, and then never looking to improve the tendon: that is existing. One could choose to no longer overstrain the tendon and hope that it just stays uninjured for the rest of life. But there are residual effects from this. This mindset of trying to not injure it again through avoidance results in quitting fun activities, avoiding opportunities for new adventures, and becoming bitter about one's lot in life. You might hear, "Oh, I can't do that anymore because I don't want to reinjure my Achilles." It's a defeatist attitude, even though the goal is just maintaining the status quo.

Thriving, on the other hand, would mean that after recovery one can actually be in better condition. I learned what controls injuries to the Achilles and how to prevent and mitigate them. I started running again; however, I made changes.

- I bought running shoes that were better fitting and suited to the type of running I was doing.
- I read about how to properly stride to avoid injuries of any type. Turns out, my stride was wrong and probably a catalyst to, or at least a culprit of, the injury.
- I changed my goals and objectives from speed and distance to technique and sustainability.
- I listened to my body and stopped "pushing" when it was clearly time to stop.
- I chose to keep learning.
- I made better decisions in the short term to benefit sustainability.

Here's a quick example of one of the results of knowledge and decision-making for me: I was playing golf in Palm Springs with my golf buddies from high school. We were playing a very hilly course with frequent elevation changes. Even though we were in a cart, going to and from the green required walking through hilly spots. I soon realized my Achilles tendon was not going to respond well to the hills because of their extreme arch. Instead of bailing, I knew that if I walked backwards up the steep slopes, my Achilles wouldn't be taxed in the same way, *plus* (this is the thriving part) I would give extra exercise to my quadriceps. I found a way to not only survive but also thrive out of a situation that might have caused me additional pain and injury.

How can you take this concept and apply it to your business and those you lead?

- A fire burns a building to the ground. Existing is simply building a similar building in its place and picking up where you left off. Thriving is creating a new experience for your customers by adding new value and creativity. You might build a unique, state-of-the-art facility that makes the old place look ancient. You thrive.

- A competitor moves in across the street, threatening to hurt your sales. Instead of "playing for par" and keeping those you already have as customers, you engage in a new tactic of setting yourself apart from your competitor. You create (see a trend?); you invest in your products/service/people; you aggressively seek out new customers with innovation. You thrive.

- Gossip, drama, and conflict have swooped into your ranks and your employee morale is in the toilet. You can simply try to allay the damage by holding staff meetings to air grievances, meeting with individuals and begging them to change, or even just trying to not add to the drama itself. *Or* you can assess whether you're the proximate cause of the problems. You can hire experts to help you identify problems and implement solutions. You can determine if there are folks who can't be developed because they have their own agendas and might have to be asked to leave. You can begin creating a new culture that has increased communications and certainty. That's thriving.

Your turn: What's the most challenging issue you've had to deal with in the last thirty days, either professionally or personally? What did you do to handle it? Are you better off today than you were before, or are you just on the same path? Are you just hoarding lemons, or are you making lemonade?

As a leader, you can't get so myopic in the weeds of the issues that you divest yourself of responsibility for being part of the problem. Unleashed leaders are always looking to grow, especially out of a crisis situation. Silver linings are nice, but you want more than just nice. You want that pot at the end of the rainbow.

Legendary professional golfer Bobby Jones once quipped that the toughest golf game one will ever face is played on the five-and-a-half-inch course located between your ears. Likewise, professional opportunities and challenges all are played out in those same five and a half inches. Your thoughts, your words, and your mindset will be responsible for your outcomes. They will be responsible for your opportunities, for the success and failure of your team and your business. And they will be the catalysts to how you view your life and what lifestyle you want to live. Alan Weiss repeatedly reminds us that we don't have a personal life and a professional life. We have a life. Do to advances in technology, those two are intertwined more than ever. You can set goals, or you can decide to achieve. You can survive, or you can thrive. The choices are yours.

AIG took a huge reputation hit when the economy imploded. The financial giant had to be saved by the government to avoid an even greater financial mess. While the AIG investment and real estate portfolio was the culprit, their insurance business was actually quite solid.

Unfortunately for them, insurance clients didn't see the difference, and their insurance business got slaughtered. In an effort to divest that perception and loss of reputation, AIG tried a new name for their insurance division, Chartis. Just like "New Coke" twenty years earlier, the switch was a flop. They quickly went back to their old AIG name and revamped how they marketed and what their message was. They enhanced their offerings, rolled out innovative ideas to help their clients, and literally changed their image rather than their name. It worked, and AIG is once again a giant in the industry. In fact, they are better than they were before. That's thriving.

Unleashed Leadership
The Wrap Up

Mindset is critical. There is a significant difference between *setting goals* and *deciding* to do something. Setting goals implies that a goal might or might not be met. While meeting goals might reach certain objectives, that goal-oriented mindset always has an element of negativity associated with it.

Deciding to do something is a different animal. Deciding to take action, to implement, to change, or to improve means there is no chance of not meeting or attaining something because you've made a decision and committed to doing it.

Example: *My goal* would be to get through the next year without injuring my Achilles heel. *My decision* is to research ways to not only heal more quickly, but also to make it better than it ever was.

Example: *My goal* is to make this putt. *My decision* is to make a good swing.

Example: *My goal* is to double my income. *My decision* is to make three new calls a day to prospective clients.

Example: *My goal* is to get everyone to play nice together so I don't have to waste time being referee. *My decision* is to change the culture though internal and external means.

Example: *My goal* is to retire in five years. *My decision* is to enjoy every single day that I work and get the most out of it.

Life is about events that you both control and don't control. Living is about your mindset. This entire book really revolves about what you say to yourself and how you decide to live. We need to remember that we have more control than we think, and what we say to ourselves is often more important than what others say to us.

Extra Point: I've always loved the words from that famous intergalactic philosopher, Yoda. He said, "Do. . .or do not. There is no try." Now *that* is a mindset.

My first job was as a personal lines underwriter for an insurance company. When I interviewed for the job, I really had no idea what an underwriter was. It sounded eerily like an undertaker, so I was a bit dubious. I soon learned that an underwriter is the person in an insurance transaction that gets to make the big decision. They get to say yes or no to accepting someone's auto or homeowners insurance application. You see, Jane and Joe Smith go to the local insurance agent and ask to get auto insurance. They dutifully complete an application as the agent smiles at them and assures them they will make fine clients. The agent then sends the new application into the company where an underwriter reviews the application to determine acceptability. Simple, right?

Not so much for me. I had the mindset of saying yes, while it became apparent that the company wanted me to be more, let's say, cynical. One time, I approved a new auto policy for a twenty-two-year-old woman who had just graduated from college and gotten her first job. She had no accidents or tickets on her driving record. Our agent personally called me to vouch for her because he insured the family through our company. This all seemed like a slam-dunk to me, so I said yes.

I soon was ushered into my boss's office along with my frowning supervisor. I had overstepped my boundary. Her age and lack of experience (in the job market—she had a 3.8 GPA in college) made her a default no, and at best, insured in the less standard market so she could pay more money. My boss wanted me to call the agent to tell him that we could keep her, but only at a much higher rate.

I was shocked. I gave all my supporting evidence, but it fell on deaf ears. While all that information seemed okay, I was making exceptions. I was playing outside of the sandbox. As I sat there, I realized that based on their argument, a monkey could do the job. If I wasn't able to make decisions based on information, what was the use of the position? That was when I first realized I was in the wrong job!

(Note: That company no longer exists. I know many smart and professional underwriters who do a tremendous job. Underwriters need not be monkeys. . .we still need them!)

I wanted to find a way to make it work, even if it meant breaking self-imposed boundaries and practices. I realized that my nature was to find a way. In the classic movie *Jurassic Park*, actor Jeff Goldblum's character tells anyone who will listen that "Life finds a way." I wanted to find a way. . .

So should you. You've made it to the end of this book and have taken in a lot of information and opinions from me. In the end, perhaps the most important advice I can bestow on you now to thrive as an entrepreneur, executive, and leader is to seek out ways to make things that should work to work.

Too many people give up too quickly. They are fearful of consequences and what others might think. They blame others for their lot in life. They are often bitter and unfriendly. They don't look to make things work, they just want to exist.

You are different. You are reading this book because at some level you've chosen a leadership path. Sometimes, we just want to be reminded of what we need to say to ourselves and how we need to view the world. One of the things I've gained from owning four dogs is that they just want to find a way to make life work. They will find a way to get that food, to track down that snake, or to get that pillow fluffed just right. And if today it fails, tomorrow it won't.

My final thoughts to you in this book are to find a way to say yes. Find a way to fulfill your dreams by deciding to become not just successful, but also significant. Find your place and your way as an Unleashed leader. Then bring others along with you for the ride!

A Captain Jack Extra Point
No Fear

I watch television. A lot. You see I am easily entertained. I'm constantly on the lookout for other dogs to bark at. The only reason I do it is because Dan thinks it's weird. I act like I'm insulted by their presence. I make a huge commotion and sometimes even attack the television. It's up above me on a table, so I get the opportunity to show off my jumping skills. I can also learn a great deal about humans from television. (My observations of human behavior come from television because otherwise it's just Dan and the family.

That's too small a sample size.) It's not pretty. . .

Here's what I observe: humans use the emotion of fear in the wrong way. We dogs can be fearful when it makes sense. For example, if we see a car approaching us, we are afraid of getting hit so we move out of the way. If we hear noises that make us think an enemy is near, we find refuge for fear of being injured. If we feel cold, we immediately find the nearest blanket for fear of freezing our butts off!

I don't fear the dogs on television. . . I bark at them. I don't even fear dogs that are bigger than me. I bark at them too (the little ones are simply an annoyance and not worth the effort). I also don't fear freedom because adventure and opportunity come as part of it. A lot of humans fear freedom even though they say they want it. I don't know why.

Humans fear freedom when they choose to doubt their own talent. They think they might not be good enough, so they choose to recoil and withdraw just like a snake when I'm after it. Humans fear freedom when they choose to avoid the open gates in their lives—new job opportunities and advancement, entrepreneurship, writing a book (like me), and speaking publicly, to name just a few. They fear freedom when they choose not to say something that needs to be said or do something that needs to be done, choose to compare themselves to others, or think too small due to lack of self-esteem. Heck, I've barked at Great Danes before. No other dog scares me!

Maybe when humans watch TV they should take a larger view than mere entertainment. Maybe they should pretend they are looking in a mirror and find ways they can emulate those that they like because they are fearless. They can then start being more fearless themselves. Bark on.

> *Just saying. . .*
> Captain Jack

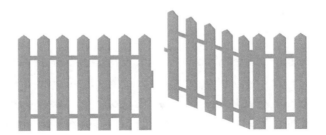

Author Bio

Dan Weedin is an expert in strategic leadership. He helps executives and entrepreneurs build dynamic and resilient organizations while maximizing the talents and skills of everyone in the organization. He founded Toro Consulting, Inc., in 2005 and regularly presents to international groups on the topics of leadership and organizational performance. Dan lives near Seattle, WA, with his wife, Barb, and their two canine companions, Captain Jack and Bella.